A
STUDENT HANDBOOK
OF LATIN AND ENGLISH
GRAMMAR

A
STUDENT HANDBOOK
OF LATIN AND ENGLISH
GRAMMAR

PETER L. CORRIGAN
and
ROBERT MONDI

Hackett Publishing Company, Inc.
Indianapolis/Cambridge

17 16 15 14   1 2 3 4 5 6 7

For further information, please address
Hackett Publishing Company, Inc.
P.O. Box 44937
Indianapolis, Indiana 46244-0937

www.hackettpublishing.com

Cover design by Ryan Picazio
Interior design by Elizabeth L. Wilson
Composition by William Hartman

Library of Congress Cataloging-in-Publication Data
Corrigan, Peter L., author.
    A student handbook of Latin and English grammar /
Peter L. Corrigan and Robert Mondi.
        pages cm
    Includes bibliographical references and index.
    ISBN 978-1-62466-130-3 (pbk.) — ISBN 978-1-62466-131-0 (cloth)
    1. Latin language—Grammar. 2. English language—Grammar.
I. Mondi, Robert Joseph, author. II. Title.
    PA2080.2.C67 2014
    478.2421—dc23   2013046588

This book is dedicated to all our students.

CONTENTS

III. The Syntax of Verbs and Related Elements

PREFACE

Primary language acquisition is one of the most miraculous achievements of the human organism. Within the first few years of life, and seemingly without conscious effort, a child internalizes one of the most complex mental structures that he or she will ever learn. Furthermore, the degree to which children learn to speak "correctly" (i.e., according to the formal rules of grammar for the language being spoken) depends primarily on the correctness of the particular speakers they are imitating. So most children eventually learn not to say things like "more big" or "beautifuler," since few adults commit these grammatical errors. But if you were to ask not only children, but even most adults, what the "rule" is in English for adjectival comparison, the initial reaction would in most cases be hesitation and uncertainty. Those who eventually arrive at the correct formulation will generally do so by going through specific examples in their minds and deducing the rule empirically from what they just 'know' to be right or wrong.

All of which is to say that by the time it takes place (if it ever does), the formal study of the grammar of one's first language is largely descriptive rather than prescriptive—not learning *how* to say things, but rather *why* we say them as we do. By the time children are old enough to study the grammar of their own language, they already know how to speak it, and for the most part correctly, in accordance with rules that they perhaps cannot articulate but observe consistently. So what is the point of such study? True, it can help elucidate certain fine points of formally correct speech, ones that are rendered less transparent by the fact that so many speakers misapply them. So, for example, the student of grammar will learn why it is correct to say (at least grammatically, if not always contextually) things like "this is she," and to avoid the hypercorrect "between you and I." He or she may also learn how to avoid the common syntactic pitfall of non-agreement of subject and verb in sentences where they are widely separated. Do such sporadic benefits justify subjecting generations of school children to the comprehensive study of English grammar, as has been traditionally done?

Many modern educators have apparently answered this question in the negative. A minority of students entering college today will claim to have been taught formal grammar in high school, and the widespread ignorance of grammatical terms like "participle" or "gerund" substantiates their claim. Whether this negatively impacts their effective use of English is perhaps debatable; what is beyond debate is a severe loss on another front—the study of a foreign language, especially the classical languages. For here the learning is indeed prescriptive. Students must learn the rules governing how Romans and Greeks said things in order to translate what they said into English. And those rules are of necessity expressed in the abstract language of grammatical terminology. So those who earlier in their education escaped the grammatical study of English now pay the price: they must learn the principles of grammar in general at the same time that they are learning the grammar of Latin or Greek in particular. What makes this situation doubly unfortunate is that the traditional presentation of English grammar in schools was heavily based on grammatical categories drawn from the classical languages. So the fact that they were already familiar with precisely those grammatical terms and constructions that they would need for the study of the classical languages greatly facilitated these earlier generations of students, already well versed in English grammar, in their study of Latin and Greek. Consequently, older textbooks took for granted this basic linguistic competence on the part of the student and focused exclusively on the grammar of Latin and Greek. They are, needless to say, all but unusable in the modern American classroom.

This book is an attempt to remedy this situation for today's students of classical Latin. Although most recent Latin textbooks do recognize that things have changed, and presume little or no previous linguistic experience on the part of the student, their remediation often amounts to little more than providing definitions of grammatical terminology. We present a fuller explanation and illustration of every grammatical entity, from the most basic to the most complex, first as it occurs in English and then in Latin. Our hope thereby is that the student will fully understand each item of grammar in and of itself, before seeing just how the Latin is or is not similar to the English. As a collateral benefit, the students will acquire a facility with the grammar of their own language, and come to know just why, for example, it is wrong to say "between you and I."

* * * * * * * *

We are pleased to acknowledge our gratitude to Dr. James C. McKeown of the University of Wisconsin at Madison for his careful reading of the penultimate draft of this text and his useful suggestions. It was a great pleasure for us to work with Mr. Brian Rak and Ms. Liz Wilson of Hackett Publishing to bring this book to completion; their input on key decisions proved invaluable, and we are most grateful to them both for their patience, professionalism, and generosity.

* * * * * * * *

At nearly every college and university across the country, Latin is offered within a classics or a world languages department as part of a larger liberal arts curriculum. The Latin etymon for "liberal" is, of course, *liberare* "to free." When Thomas Jefferson, one of the greatest advocates for freedom of thought in the history of North America, was called on to found the institution that would become the University of Virginia, he envisioned the classical languages at the very center of the liberal arts curriculum. He understood, better perhaps than we do today, that the study of Latin is one of the greatest acts we can perform toward the goals of self-liberation and engaged citizenship. "To read the Latin and Greek authors in their original is a sublime luxury. . . . I thank on my knees him who directed my early education for having in my possession this rich source of delight; and I would not exchange it for anything which I could then have acquired, & have not since acquired" (Thomas Jefferson in a letter to Dr. Joseph Priestley, January 27, 1800).

Peter L. Corrigan

Robert Mondi

January 2014

INTRODUCTION

REMARKS FOR INSTRUCTORS

Students enrolling in beginning courses in classical Latin today bring with them the widest possible range of previous linguistic experience. For those with experience in some other foreign language (especially a European one), at the very least such concepts as verb conjugation, noun gender, and noun-adjective agreement will be familiar. But even these fundamental ideas might be alien to the student approaching Latin as a first foreign language (a less rare occurrence than one might think). Consequently, as regards syntax and morphology English can fairly be said to be, among European languages at any rate, the worst starting point for the study of Latin or Greek. Confronted with this situation, we have opted to take the grammatical competence (or lack thereof) of this final group as our baseline and to define, explain, and illustrate even the most elementary terms and concepts, thinking that it is preferable for you to advise students to skip over what they already know rather than have to supplement what is here with further remedial explanations of your own.

We assume that this book will be used as a companion to whatever primary Latin textbook you are using in your course. In an ideal world, the topics in such an auxiliary resource would be arranged in the same order as they appear in the textbook. Since, however, there is such wide variety in the order of presentation in various beginning Latin textbooks commonly in use, this cannot be the case. Our decision was to present the material in the order traditionally employed in the reference grammars of the classical languages. This choice calls attention to the two-fold purpose that we envision this book can serve.

First and foremost, our intention is to introduce and/or reinforce the numerous grammatical concepts that your students will need in their study of classical Latin. This is done by first defining and then illustrating in English—to the extent that this is possible—every such concept, from the most basic to the most advanced. To this end, the organizing principle of each chapter or section is, "English first." This is true of the book overall, in that the initial section, "Preliminaries," draws solely on English to explain these most basic units of grammar, before any mention of Latin. Similarly, within each chapter dealing with a specific point of grammar, we first illustrate it with English examples and then go on to the Latin.

One way our presentation might differ from that of some introductory texts is that the latter often present the many uses of a grammatical entity in a piecemeal fashion, spread over several chapters. The subjunctive mood, for example, or the ablative case might be introduced along with one or two of the most common uses, with the rest added sporadically in subsequent chapters. We here present all of the most important applications of a grammatical category at the time the category is introduced, thus enabling the student to get an overview of its syntactic range—a feeling for its linguistic "logic," so to speak. Many of these uses will be revisited in subsequent chapters (cross references will point the way). So the use of the subjunctive in purpose and result clauses will be noted when this verbal mood is first introduced and then again later in the chapters on the various types of clauses that employ it. Consequently, we do not expect that the chapters of this book will be covered sequentially, as would those of a primary textbook, but rather that you will call attention to the relevant sections where appropriate.

A second potential use we see for this text is as a reference work, filling the gap between the introductory text used in the beginning course, and the standard reference grammars, such as those of Gildersleeve and Lodge or Allen and Greenough. The latter offer far too much information for the beginning or intermediate student, even if they are available; but the former is often difficult to use as a reference tool for precisely the reason noted above: material is organized for purposes of pedagogy, not reference. So the second-year student who wants, perhaps, to review the different uses of the ablative case or the variety of Latin pronouns will find them here conveniently gathered in one place, thus obviating the need to haul out the old introductory text and seek out all the places where these things are to be found separately (if they are there at all). You will quickly see that we have in places included more detailed information than the beginner will be able to digest, but this will be of use to the more advanced student. This is particularly true of those sections we have set off in the text as "Fine Points." Here too, we assume that you will direct the students' attention to the sections that are appropriate to each level of study.

We have included no exercises in the text. For the Latin, these will presumably be found in the textbook you are using. We do recommend that you on occasion create English exercises of your own to test the students' grasp in their own language of some of the topics that commonly present problems, such as relative clauses and participles, before turning to the Latin. You might, for example, give them pairs of short sentences and ask them to combine them into single sentences using active and passive participles, or relative clauses eschewing the universal "that" and requiring a choice of who, whom, which, or whose. Another useful and easily prepared exercise is to give students a page of English text (it can be anything) and ask them to do such things as underline all participles and indicate which noun they modify; indicate any subjunctive verbs that might appear; or state which case a given noun would be in if the passage were to be translated into Latin. Even if translation from English to Latin is not part of your pedagogical approach, this can be a beneficial activity.

REMARKS FOR STUDENTS

Trying to make sense out of language is a little like trying to catch sight of yourself blinking. The best tool for making sense of language is language itself, but when we use language, we tend to do so quite unselfconsciously. Language seems to come naturally to us. Like blinking.

For most Americans, just about the time when we're starting to feel pretty confident and competent with our first language, we're often thrown into a second. And if that second language is largely unspoken, like classical Latin, we're asked to think fairly analytically about language in some unfamiliar ways. Classical Latin is to native English what calculus is to arithmetic: most of the elements were there all along, but they're now applied in some striking and novel manners.

And like calculus again, Latin isn't easy. That simple truth cannot be white-washed. Some foreign languages (ancient Greek, for example) are hardest at the beginning level; classical Latin is hardest at the intermediate. It is the intention of this book to make learning Latin easier for you by comparing it most closely to the language you already know: English. By understanding this comparison better, you can free up your brain to do more of the mechanical tasks of learning Latin vocabulary and morphology ("endings").

Though it may seem otherwise, the study of grammar is actually 'glamor-ous'. If you look up the words "grammar" and "glamour" in an etymological dictionary, you'll discover that they are derived from the same Greek word meaning "letter." You'll also notice a definition for the former that reads something like this: that field of linguistic study that pertains to a language's inflectional forms or other means of specifying the relations of words within the phrase, clause, or sentence, and with the rules for using these in conformity with standard or established usage. So wear your newfound learning like the fine and stylish look that it is!

This is what we think is the best and most productive procedure for using this book. When you are assigned to read a section of this book, concentrate first on English usage. Make sure you clearly understand how the English works within the assigned section. Only after you've secured that understanding should you analyze how the corresponding Latin works. At that point you can make special note of both the commonalities and the differences—now you're achieving a basic competency. But the next step brings you to true proficiency: grasping the fine points of a language. We will provide you with sufficient basics and fine points in this book to sophisticate your knowledge of both Latin and English.

A second valuable use for this volume is ongoing review and recovery—a process you should be continually engaged in. The more times you review grammatical concepts the firmer they'll be fixed in your active comprehension. So peruse this book often; and those sections containing more difficult concepts you should peruse even more often.

This book is only one part of an essential learning troika for you. The second part is your instructor: she or he will clarify any uncertainties for you and provide other examples to reinforce our basic observations. If something you read here really piques your curiosity, your instructor can assist you with reference works that allow you to plumb deeper. The third part of the troika is your main Latin text, which this volume is only meant to supplement. Your main text supplies all foreground, while this book offers only background. The two books together can provide you with all the information you need, so that with every new point of Latin grammar you can confidently claim, "Ah-ha! I really get it now."

A supplement not only to your elementary Latin textbook, this volume can also be used later in conjunction with your intermediate text and your first advanced texts. Indeed, this can serve you until you're at home with the more comprehensive grammars cited below. The point is: consult this book whenever you're exposed to a linguistic concept or a technical term that baffles you in English as much as in Latin. By having the familiar explained to you, the foreign should seem much less foreign. And in the long run, your love and admiration for classical Latin will only increase as you recognize it for a far more straightforward historical and cultural artifact than the language you happen to speak.

SUGGESTIONS FOR FURTHER READING

The most accessible modern grammars of English are:

Aarts, Bas, *Oxford Modern English Grammar,* Oxford University Press, Oxford and New York, 2011.

Huddleston, Rodney, and Geoffrey K. Pullum, *The Cambridge Grammar of the English Language,* Cambridge University Press, Cambridge and New York, 2002.

A fun and fascinating read can be found with this classic:

Fowler, W. H., *A Dictionary of Modern English Usage* (3rd edition revised by R. W. Burchfield), Oxford University Press, Oxford and New York, 2004 (first published 1906).

For an historical overview of Latin, see:

Clackson, James, and Geoffrey Horrocks, *The Blackwell History of the Latin Language*, Blackwell, Oxford, 2007.

Janson, Tore, *A Natural History of Latin*, Oxford University Press, Oxford and New York, 2004.

If you are interested in how classical Latin was probably spoken, you can refer to:

Allen, W. Sidney, *Vox Latina: The Pronunciation of Classical Latin* (2nd edition), Cambridge University Press, Cambridge and New York, 1978 (first published 1965).

Among standard Latin reference grammars, the more accessible are:

Hale, William G., and Carl D. Buck, *A Latin Grammar*, University of Alabama Press, Tuscaloosa, 1966 (first published 1903).

Gildersleeve, B. L., and Gonzalez Lodge, *Gildersleeve's Latin Grammar*, Dover Publications, Mineola, 2009 (first published 1867).

Allen, J. H., and James B. Greenough, *Allen and Greenough's New Latin Grammar*, Dover Publications, Mineola, 2006 (first published 1903).

Morwood, James, *A Latin Grammar*, Oxford University Press, Oxford and New York, 2000.

To date, the only comprehensive grammar of classical Latin in English is:

Roby, Henry John, *Grammar of the Latin Language from Plautus to Suetonius*, Cambridge University Press, Cambridge and New York, 2010 (first published 1872–1881).

Most or all of these books can be found in your college's or university's library.

I. PRELIMINARIES

1. INFLECTION

In American English, the word inflection usually refers to the tone with which a word or phrase is uttered.

But in Latin (and many other languages), **inflection** refers to the affixes added to word roots (of nouns, verbs, adjectives, and pronouns) to specify their function within a sentence, clause, or phrase. An **affix** is any semantically meaningful element added to a word root.

The husband reads the book.

Father's horses helped them.

I had competed very proudly.

maritus librum legit.

equi patris eos adiuvabant.

gloriosissime certaveram.

Thus, we meet a very important axiom for translating Latin: *function follows form.* That is, the form (also called **morphology**) that a Latin word takes with respect to its inflection(s) points to its specific grammatical function. Therefore, the more thoroughly you learn the inflections of Latin, the better you'll be enabled to translate.

Suffixes (affixes added to the end of a word root) and **prefixes** (affixes added to the beginning of a word root) constitute the standard affixes in English:

unsupported

In addition to these, Latin also employs **infixes** (i.e., inflectional elements of significance placed within words).

vere<u>bi</u>mur: we <u>will</u> fear

Far and away, though, suffixes are the most common and most important inflectional element of Latin word formation.[1]

Latin's reliance on inflection to indicate grammatical function carries a consequence that's sometimes hard to adjust to, especially at first: typically, Latin isn't read strictly from left to right as English is. Therefore, try to get into the habit of reading not word-by-word and left-to-right but by properly identifying the inflections on words and by isolating semantically linked phrases and clauses.

Some older grammar books occasionally refer to morphology and inflectional endings as **accidence**.

---

1. For nonstandard English, consider the word unfreakingbelievable, which exhibits a prefix (un-), an infix (-freaking-), and a suffix (-able).

2. PARTS OF SPEECH

2.1 NOUNS

A **noun** is a word that refers to a person, place, concrete object, or abstract idea. If it refers to only one such entity, it is a **singular noun**; if more than one, a **plural noun**.

> The shepherd guards his flocks on the mountainside.

> Philosophy teaches us to live the good life.

If the noun is the name of someone or something, it is a **proper noun**:

> Caesar was a populist leader in Rome.

If not, it is a **common noun**:

> Caesar was a populist leader in the city.

A noun used as a **complement** (i.e., as a word needed to complete the sense of another word or phrase) after a linking verb (see §2.6 below) is called a **predicate noun**:

> Seneca was a critic of the Epicureans.

> Seneca remains an inspiration for those in search of the truth.

Some grammar books use the word **substantive** to designate a noun or any other part of speech (e.g., an adjective or verb) being used as a noun.

2.2 ADJECTIVES

An **adjective** is a word that characterizes or describes a noun.

> The angry Romans launched many ships to rescue the abducted queen.

> Safe at last, the sailors made an offering to the gods.

> Panting, the messenger reported that the Romans had been defeated at Cannae.

3

Sometimes the adjective may appear after linking verbs, in which case it is called a **predicate adjective**.

This orator is eloquent.

The children seem happy.

I became angry.

Demonstrative adjectives express the relative closeness of a noun to the speaker.

These verses are inferior to those poems written by the ancient poets.

That army will never conquer this city.

2.3 ARTICLES

When used with a noun, the **definite article** marks it as specific or unique.

The king of Parthia led his army against the Romans.

Seneca was the philosopher who spoke the truth.

The **indefinite article** marks the noun as merely a member of a class or category.

A king of Parthia is someone to be feared.

Seneca was a philosopher who spoke the truth.

2.4 PRONOUNS

A pronoun is a word used in place of a noun. **Personal pronouns** are employed when both speaker and listener presumably know who is being referred to. In the case of a **1st-person pronoun** ("I"/"we"), the referent is (or includes) the speaker, and in that of a **2nd-person pronoun** ("you"), it is (or includes) the listener.

I can see you, but you can't see me.

We learn truth through suffering.

Third-person pronouns refer to things or persons other than the speaker or listener, and their referents are therefore not self-evident. They generally refer to something or someone mentioned previously and thus eliminate the need for repetition.

The Romans listened to the Gallic herald, but <u>they</u> did not believe <u>him</u>.

I read that book, but I did not understand <u>it</u>.

Interrogative pronouns are used in questions, which can be either direct or indirect.

<u>Who</u> is making that noise?

I know <u>what</u> you did.

Indefinite pronouns imply an ignorance of their precise referent.

<u>Someone</u> is sneaking through the gate.

I know you are hiding <u>something</u> from me.

Relative pronouns introduce clauses that characterize a noun or pronoun located elsewhere in the sentence.

We can't trust a man <u>who</u> talks of peace but prepares for war.

He <u>whom</u> the gods love dies young.

2.5 PREPOSITIONS

A **preposition** is a word used in a phrase with a noun (or other substantive) expressing that noun's relationship to another word or idea.

Few citizens came <u>to</u> the assembly.
(prepositional phrase: 'to the assembly')

We sat <u>in</u> the theater all day.
(prepositional phrase: 'in the theater')

Octavia was praised <u>by</u> the philosophers.
(prepositional phrase: 'by the philosophers')

Scipio left <u>with</u> them.
(prepositional phrase: 'with them')

2.6 VERBS

The word that expresses the acting, being, doing, or the like connecting the subject to the predicate in a clause or sentence is called a **verb**.

Ulysses <u>wandered</u> for ten years.

Caesar <u>is</u> our leader.

Verbs that do not express a particular action but describe or define the subject are called **linking verbs**:

Fabius Maximus <u>is</u> our leader.

The athletes <u>seem</u> tired.

Augustus has <u>become</u> quite old.

In English, a verb can be accompanied by one or more **auxiliary verbs**.

Juno <u>will be</u> <u>honored</u> by this. (the verb 'honor' is being augmented by the auxiliary verbs 'will' and 'be')

2.7 PARTICLES

A **particle** is a word (or pseudoword, so to speak) added to convey earnestness, hesitation, uncertainty, doubt, or equivocation. While it is possible for particles to be omitted grammatically, semantically they add tone, coloration, and nuance, especially in rhetorical and/or conversational settings.

That woman is a, <u>er</u>, friend of mine.

<u>Um</u>, let me think about that for a moment.

It's a beautiful statue, <u>eh</u>?

<u>Ah</u>, those were the days!

The answer to that question, <u>well</u>, we may never know.

It's about, <u>hmm</u>, three miles from here.

2.8 CONJUNCTIONS

A word that links two or more grammatically equivalent parts is a **conjunction**.

Agrippa <u>and</u> Maecenas were his friends.
(linking nouns)

Tomorrow, they will fight <u>or</u> withdraw.
(linking verbs)

Lucullus was severe <u>but</u> just.
(linking adjectives)

The Romans will resist <u>if</u> the Parthians attack.
(linking clauses)

2.9 INTERJECTIONS

An **interjection** is a word or phrase said in exclamation, independent from its grammatical or syntactic context.

My wife—<u>alas!</u>—is dead.

<u>Damn!</u> I lost that bet.

<u>O Neptune!</u> What rotten luck!

2.10 ADVERBS

We define an adverb as a word that can modify a verb, an adjective, or another adverb.

Caesar was <u>very</u> persuasive.
(modifying an adjective)

He spoke <u>very</u> clearly.
(modifying another adverb)

We <u>eagerly</u> listened to him.
(modifying a verb)

Generally, English adverbs express temporal (i.e., pertaining to time) or locative (i.e., pertaining to location) relations, manner, or degree.

3. SENTENCES, CLAUSES, AND PHRASES

3.1 SENTENCES

In practice, these parts of speech discussed in §2 are combined to produce sentences. A **sentence** is a unit of speech that is syntactically self-contained, consisting minimally of a **subject** (stated or implied), usually a noun or a pronoun telling what the topic of the sentence is, and a **predicate**, which says something about the subject and (in English) must at the very least contain a verb.

> <u>Nero</u> was a student of Seneca.

> <u>None of the friends of Seneca</u> thought that he was justly condemned.

In the first sentence, 'Nero' is the subject, and 'was a student of Seneca' is the predicate. In the second, 'None of the friends of Seneca' forms the subject, and 'thought that he was justly condemned' is the predicate.

3.2 CLAUSES

Like a sentence, a **clause** also has a subject and predicate but may not express a complete thought. If a sentence contains more than one clause, they are generally linked by conjunctions. Clauses that would be capable of standing by themselves as complete sentences are called **independent**; those that cannot are called **dependent** or **subordinate**. The incompleteness of a subordinate clause is often the result of an initial **subordinating conjunction** (see §28):

> Since Nero was a student of Seneca. . . .

> If none of the friends of Seneca thought that he was justly condemned. . . .

What is needed to complete the sentence is an independent clause, also referred to as the **main clause**:

> Although Nero was a student of Seneca, <u>he never mourned his death</u>.

> If none of the friends of Seneca thought that he was justly condemned, <u>why didn't they help him resist</u>?

A sentence consisting of only a main clause is called a **simple sentence**; a sentence consisting of a main clause and one or more subordinate clauses is called a **complex sentence**. A **compound sentence** is one containing two or more independent clauses linked with a **coordinating conjunction** (see §28).

If the subordinate clause itself contains a subordinate clause, the two parts of that clause are designated the **principal clause** and the **dependent clause**:

Although Nero was a student of Seneca, who was a Stoic philosopher, he never mourned his death.

In this sentence, the principal clause is "although Nero was a student of Seneca," and the dependent clause is "who was a Stoic philosopher."

3.3 PHRASES

A **phrase** is a group of words that forms a grammatical unit but lacks a subject and/or a predicate. There are various types of phrases:

Noun phrase: The victorious general was greeted as a hero.

Verb phrase: The victorious general was greeted as a hero.

Adjectival phrase: Angry at the insult, Scipio left the party.

Prepositional phrase: With hard work you will succeed in the course of time.

Participial phrase: Hastening to the city, he warned the citizens of the imminent attack.

Attacked by the barbarians, the Romans showed great valor.

Infinitive phrase: Do you want to join the feast?

Absolute phrase: Things being what they are, this is the best we can do.

The arrangement of words (with their appropriate morphology) according to their proper usage into semantically meaningful sentences, clauses, and phrases is commonly referred to as **syntax**.

II. THE SYNTAX OF NOUNS AND RELATED WORDS

4. NOUNS

As defined above (§2.1), a noun is a word that refers to a person, place, concrete object, or abstract idea. In Latin, each standard noun has three inherent characteristics: case, number, and gender. As case tends to be the most complicated of these three characteristics, we will discuss that last.

4.1 NUMBER

Number is a fairly straightforward notion in English, because English has only two numbers: **singular** (denoting one) and **plural** (denoting more than one).

The horse<u>man</u> is safe.

The horse<u>men</u> are safe.

English plurals are most commonly created with the addition of the inflection -(e)s:

tale → tales

box → boxes

Sometimes, a plural in English involves a vowel change:

goose → geese

mouse → mice

Sometimes, plurals involve a consonant change:

knife → knives

And sometimes, there is zero change in plurals:

one sheep → two sheep

one deer → two deer

Rarely, plurals exhibit the ancient Germanic plural inflection:

child → children

ox → oxen[1]

Also rare are the rather subtle distinctions English can make with plurals:

six fish = fish all of the same species

six fishes = fishes of varied species

Some **collective nouns** (i.e., nouns that denote a collection of objects, ideas, or creatures), though singular in inflection, are typically construed as grammatical plurals:

The people are satisfied.

The cattle were fed.

Note, however, that these collective nouns can sometimes be pluralized (cf. fishes, above):

The peoples of the world are satisfied.

As with English, Latin nouns are typically singular or plural:

eques est salvus.

equites sunt salvi.

The change in number is signified by changes in the noun inflections (as well as other inflections).[2]

---

1. But be careful! Chicken is not the plural of chick.

2. Indo-European, the parent language of both Latin and English, had a third number: the dual number, which expressed things that commonly or naturally occur in pairs (eyes, ears, hands, feet, parents, and twins, for example). In Latin, vestiges of the dual survive in the declensions of the words *duo* 'two' and *ambo* 'both'. In English, which lacks an actual dual number, we sometimes exhibit a grammatical uncertainty over 'duals'. For example, do you say, "A pair of corduroys is hanging in my closet" or "A

4.2 GENDER

Though they are not much in evidence, English has three grammatical genders: **masculine, feminine,** and **neuter**. Generally, these genders are determined by biology; that is, things biologically male are grammatically masculine, things biologically female are feminine, and things that have indeterminate or no biological gender are grammatically neuter. Sometimes, when certain genderless things (like ships or polities or institutions) are referred to in highly romanticized or emotionalized rhetoric, they are found in the feminine gender:

> The law is a demanding <u>mistress</u>.

> The *Andrea Doria* went down with most of <u>her</u> crew.

> Harvard College welcomed me into <u>her</u> warm embrace.

Representations of things biologically gendered can frequently employ either the corresponding gender or a neuter:

> Shakespeare's Iago is perfect: <u>he</u> is the very picture of evil.

> Shakespeare's Iago is perfect: <u>it</u> is the very picture of evil.

> This Minnie Mouse is different; <u>her</u> bow is on the left side.

> This Minnie Mouse is different; <u>its</u> bow is on the left side.

English used to employ the masculine gender as its so-called **dominant gender** for grammar, that is, as the default grammatical gender when the biological gender of a noun or pronoun was indeterminate:

> Anyone [even if the person is female] who says this should check <u>his</u> facts.

Amid considerable confusion (not to mention dubious grammar), English now commonly pluralizes personal pronouns precisely because they are gender indeterminate:

> Anyone who says this should check <u>their</u> facts.

Latin also has the three grammatical genders of masculine, feminine, and neuter. In Latin, however, grammatical gender is not simply determined by

---

pair of corduroys <u>are</u> hanging in my closet"? Similarly, which is correct: "Last spring, a couple of robins <u>was</u> nesting on our front porch" or "Last spring, a couple of robins <u>were</u> nesting on our front porch"?

biological gender: often the gender of a Latin noun is seemingly arbitrary or influenced by the gender of other nouns that it in some way resembles. In fine, apart from the names of people (who are understood as being either feminine or masculine), all other Latin nouns have a grammatical gender that is often unpredictable (and must, therefore, be learned when the noun is first introduced in vocabulary).

Latin also has the notion of dominant gender. For nouns of mixed or indeterminate gender, the masculine gender is commonly applied.

Parthi sunt barbari: The Parthians [male and female] are barbaric.

et mulieres et viri erant magni: Both the women and the men were large.

If compound abstract nouns are used in the Latin subject, often the predicate is neuter plural:

virtus et audacia et ingenium sunt utilia: Courage, daring, and intelligence are useful (things).

4.3 CASE

Indo-European, the common ancestor of Latin and English, had many different noun cases. Each case expressed a specific noun function within sentences, clauses, and phrases and was distinguished by its own proper inflections. Such functions included direct object, instrumentality, possession, subject, location, and the like.

English nouns don't really preserve the feature of case and noun function, unless one considers the use of -'s and -s' to express possession:

the book's binding

the kittens' mother

Besides the possessive case, the subjective case and the objective case are also grammatically observed in English, even though they're not inflectionally observed in nouns.

Latin preserved seven of Indo-European's main noun cases and functions, and they are identified by means of inflectional endings:

4.3.1 Nominative Case: Expresses the sentence's or clause's subject and predicate subject:

Caesar est imperator: Caesar is commander.

4.3.2 Genitive Case: Many of the uses of the genitive case in Latin can be rendered in English with the preposition "of":

Possession: *filia Ovidii:* the daughter of Ovid, Ovid's daughter

Source or material: *poculum auri:* the cup of gold

Descriptive quality: *homo magnae sapientiae:* a person of great wisdom

Part of a whole: *pars maxima urbis:* the largest part of the city
    fortissimus Romanorum: the bravest of the Romans

When used in conjunction with a noun that carries a verbal sense, the genitive can function as either the subject or the object of the action implied by the noun and is designated as either the **subjective** or the **objective genitive**, respectively:

nonne terrorem hostium sensis?
    Do you not perceive the fear of the enemy? (i.e., the enemy's fear of us: the enemy is here the subject of the idea of fearing)

terror hostium nos retinuit:
    Fear of the enemy restrained us (i.e., our fear of the enemy: the enemy is the object of the idea of fearing).

4.3.3 Dative Case: Expresses indirect object; agency in the passive periphrastics of verbs (see §15); possessor of nominative objects when used with the verb 'to be'; and other uses, as well (see §5 below):

dic haec servis: Tell (to) the slaves these things.

haec comitiis facienda sunt: These things must be done by the assembly.

erant tres equi patri: Father had three horses [literally: there were to father three horses].

4.3.4 Accusative Case: Expresses the direct object of verbs and verbal nouns and adjectives (see §11.2); the expressed subject of an infinitive (see §16.2); the objects of certain prepositions; and other uses, as well (see §5):

Seneca Agrippinam salutabat: Seneca was greeting Agrippina.

facile non est vincere Romanos: It isn't easy to defeat the Romans.

dico Romanos victuros esse: I say that the Romans will win.

trans montes et per silvas: across mountains and through woods

4.3.5 Ablative Case: Used for the object of prepositions or verbs including the sense of 'from', 'in', 'with', or 'by' and has many other uses, as well (see §5):

procul aberamus Roma: We were far from Rome.

Caesar cum Antonio pervenit: Caesar arrived with Antony.

hoc sagittis actum erat: This had been done with arrows.

The genitive, dative, accusative, and ablative cases are collectively referred to as the **oblique cases**.

4.3.6 Vocative Case: Expresses direct address and **apostrophe** (a sudden exclamatory address to a person or thing that may not even be present or real):

o Tulle: O Tullus!

ubi es, geni?: Where are you, divine guardian?

iuvate me, di: Help me, gods!

4.3.7 Locative Case: Place "where" or "at which" and used only with the names of cities, of towns, and of small islands and with the nouns *rus* 'country', *humus* 'ground', and *domus* 'home'; for all of these, prepositions are <u>not</u> employed to express location.

Romae: at Rome

Cannis: at Cannae

Rhodi: on Rhodes, at Rhodes

domi: at home

In English, because nouns don't generally exhibit case differentiation (except in the possessive), they don't behave according to much of a system of inflectional endings (**paradigm**). In Latin, each noun generally conforms and belongs to one of five consistent patterns or paradigms of inflection, called **declensions**.

In the 1st declension, the vowel -*a*- predominates in the inflections. In the 2nd declension, -*o*- and -*u*- predominate in the case inflections. In the 3rd declension, -*i*- and -*e*- predominate. The vowel -*u*- predominates in the 4th declension, while -*ei*- predominates in the 5th. If you learn the 1st and 2nd declensions thoroughly, the somewhat more difficult 3rd, 4th, and 5th declensions become relatively easier to master.

5. SPECIAL USES FOR NOUN CASES

Latin has some subtle and unique ways of expressing common ideas by means of nouns and noun phrases. The array of Latin noun cases affords the ability to make meaningful and sometimes fascinating distinctions. The locutions we survey in this chapter range from the fairly idiomatic to the highly rhetorical.

5.1 PERSONAL AGENCY

In passive constructions (see §11.5), where the action of the verb and the subject acted upon are usually the emphasis of the sentence, clause, or phrase, it is sometimes necessary also to specify the person by whom the passive action was done. In English, we do this by using the preposition 'by':

The letters were brought by slaves.

This same idea is also most often expressed by a preposition in Latin: *a* or *ab* with the ablative case. When the verb is found in a passive periphrastic (see §15), however, personal agency is expressed with a simple dative, without a preposition:

The letters were brought by his father.

epistulae a patre ferebantur.

The letters must be brought by his father.

epistulae patri ferendae sunt.

In **impersonal** constructions (i.e., when the subject of a verb is an indefinite "it"), which are quite common in Latin, personal agency is expressed according to the grammar of each construction. In constructions with neuter singular adjectives and the verb 'to be' in the 3rd person singular, the dative is used for agency:

commodum est mihi illud facere: It is convenient for me to do that.

With impersonal verbs accompanied by an infinitive, sometimes a dative or sometimes an accusative conveys agency—the idiom varies from verb to verb:

licet nobis venire: It is permitted for us to come.

non taedet me legere: It doesn't bore me to read.

accidit eis discedere: It happens that they are leaving.

oportebat te pervenire: It was necessary for you to arrive.

These examples are hardly exhaustive. Perhaps the most unusual expression of agency comes with the impersonals *refert* and *interest*, 'it is in the interest of' or 'it concerns', which can be followed either by an infinitive or an *ut*-clause; if the agent is a noun, the genitive case is used:

interest ducis discedere: It is in the leader's interest to depart.

refert feminarum ut maritos bonos eligant: It's of concern to the women to pick good husbands.

But when the agent of *refert* and *interest* is a personal or reflexive pronoun, the ablative feminine singular of the corresponding possessive adjective is used:

interest mea discedere: It is in my interest to depart.

refert vestra ut maritos bonos eligatis: It's of your concern to pick good husbands.[1]

5.2 EXCLAMATION

When we're angry, surprised, frightened, or otherwise agitated, we tend to blurt things out without much regard for the grammar or syntax of our native language; typically, however, we don't employ utter gibberish to respond to such conditions.

In a Latin exclamation involving a direct address, the vocative case is used. If respect or politeness is being expressed, the interjection *o* precedes the noun.

o Iuppiter: O Jupiter!

When the interjections *en* or *ecce*, 'behold', are used, the nominative case generally follows:

en dextera mea: Behold this right hand of mine!

ecce servi Ciceronis: Look, here are Cicero's slaves!

---

1. In the latter case, *vestra* is in fact modifying the noun *re*, which is the first part of the verb *refert*. The use of the ablative *mea* with *interest* is on analogy with *refert*.

The interjections *ei, vae,* or (sometimes) *eheu,* 'woe to' or 'alas for', can be used with an ethical dative to express an exclamation:

ei/vae <u>nobis</u>: Woe to us!

The most common construction for exclamations in Latin, however, is a simple accusative with an adjective or a genitive. In exclamations that express oaths or swearing, the vestigial interjection *pro* can be found:

o <u>me</u> miserum: O miserable me!

<u>dedecus</u> huius criminis: The disgrace of this charge!

pro <u>deos</u> <u>immortales</u>: By the immortal gods!

5.3 MEANS/MANNER/INSTRUMENT

In noun phrases that answer the question 'how?', a variety of expressions can be found. For an actual instrument or physical object, the simple ablative case is used in Latin. If the means or manner is abstract, a simple ablative is usually employed when the noun is modified by an adjective (although it is permissible for *cum* to be present); if no modifier is present, the preposition *cum* (with the ablative noun) is necessarily used:

We will do this with stones.

   hoc saxis agemus.

We will do this with much eagerness.

   hoc magno (cum) studio agemus.

We will do this with eagerness.

   hoc cum studio agemus.

Some simple nouns in the accusative case take on an almost adverbial force. These expressions, while few in number, are quite high in frequency:

clam and *clanculum:* under cover, in secret

coram: face to face, in person

foras: outside

genus: of a certain kind

nihil: not at all

palam: in the open, outwardly

partem: to an extent

partim: in part[2]

passim: here and there, at random

pessum: to the bottom, to ruin

vicem: in turn

vicissim: in turn, in order

venus: for sale

saltem: at least

secus: of a certain gender

Some adjectives used substantively (see §6.7) are construed in the same way:

alias: at another time or place

aliquam: to a considerable extent

ceterum: further, besides

cetera: in other respects

iterum: again, once more

multum: much

parum (< *parvum*): little, too little

paulum: a little

perperam: incorrectly, by mistake

perpetuum: constantly, forever

---

2. There is a very large class of denominative adverbs like *partim* ending in *-im*, the oldest of which were adverbial accusatives; this class includes words like *vicissim* 'in turn', 'for a change'; *viritim* 'per person', 'individually'; *verbatim* 'word for word'; *serietim* 'serially'; etc. Later, the *-im* suffix was added to the 4th principal part of certain verbs to make adverbs: *cessim* 'so as to lose ground'; *expulsim* 'by pushing away'; *passim* 'here and there', 'at random'; *saltuatim* 'in leaps'; *separatim* 'separately', 'individually', 'in particular'; *taxim* 'tentatively'; etc.

plerum and *plerumque:* mostly, generally

plurimum: very much

plus: to a greater extent, more

primum: first, at first, in the first place

reliqua: further, so on

solum: only

supremum: for the last time

tantum: so much

verum: but actually[3]

5.4 PRICE/VALUE

Latin has several common ways to express the cost at which objects are bought, sold, or valued. When something (or someone) is being appraised or valued, the simple genitive case of an adjective used substantively is typically used to express indefinite value; for example,

> I have a horse of great value.
>
> *equum magni habeo.*

An ablative of price is used to express more specificity (i.e., with a noun and adjective):

> I bought the horse for 100 denarii.
>
> *equum centum denariis emi.*

Occasionally the preposition *pro* with the ablative case is used:

> He sold away his country in return for gold.
>
> *patriam pro auro vendidit.*

---

3. To be included in this group are the directional adverbs: *deorsum* 'downward'; *introrsum* 'inward'; *introversum* 'toward inside'; *sursum* 'upward'; *undiqueversum* 'in every direction'; *utroversum* 'in both directions'.

An ablative of means (cf. above) or of specification can also be used in this setting; e.g.,

I will work at [the price of] 20 denarii.
viginti denariis laborabo.

This construction obviously bears great resemblance to the ablative of price.

Finally, a genitive of definite measurement can be used with words like *pretium* and *merces:*

I sold the horse at a price of 100 denarii.
equum pretio centum denariorum vendidi.

5.5 TIME EXPRESSIONS

Most expressions of time in English employ prepositional phrases:

He hid in the forest for three days.

We will see you on Saturday.

The job will be done in September.

The play starts at eight o'clock.

I will call you within a week.

In Latin, it is commonly a noun or noun phrase alone that expresses an interval or point in time, without prepositions. The accusative and ablative cases may be so used.

To specify the time when or at which something takes place, the ablative case is employed.

nuntius tertio die pervenit.
The messenger arrived on the third day.

To indicate the duration of an event or action, the accusative case is employed.

exercitus tres dies pugnabant.
The armies were fighting for three days.

The ablative case indicates the <u>time within which</u> something takes place.

hostes <u>tribus diebus</u> vincemus.
We will defeat the enemy within three days.

The use of prepositions in temporal contexts can express subtle nuance:

ad/sub noctem pervenit.
He arrived around nighttime.

in nocte pervenit.
He arrived in the dead of night.

per decem dies manebat.
He stayed specifically for ten days.

5.6 COMPARISON

English employs the conjunction 'than' to introduce the second element of a comparison:

The teacher is wiser than the student.

In the event that this element is a personal pronoun, where English still preserves case distinctions, it properly must be in the same case as the item to which it is being compared:

My brother is taller than <u>I</u>.

People love my brother more than <u>me</u> [i.e., more than they love me].

My brother's house is bigger than <u>mine</u>.

Latin syntax provides a choice of two ways of expressing such comparisons. One is precisely the same as the English construction, using the Latin conjunction *quam:*

magister est sapientior quam discipulus.
The teacher is wiser than the student.

credimus magistro magis quam discipulo.
We trust the teacher more than [we trust] the student.

credimus magistro magis quam discipulus.
We trust the teacher more than the student [trusts the teacher].

Since all nouns in Latin show case distinction, the noun following the conjunction will be in the same case as the item it is being compared to. One result of this is that the Latin comparison will lack the ambiguity that might be present in the English, as the second and third examples illustrate.

The other option in Latin is to eliminate the conjunction *quam* and put the noun that would follow it into the ablative case.

> *magister est sapientior discipulo*

This option, it should be noted, can introduce the same ambiguity into the Latin comparison as is present in the English.

In order to express the **degree of difference** involved in the comparison, a word expressing quantity or extent can be placed in the ablative case:

> *magister est multo sapientior discipulo.*
> The teacher is much wiser than the student.

> *credimus magistro tanto magis quam discipulo.*
> We trust the teacher so much more than the student.

Finally, in expressions involving the superlative degree of the adjective, the genitive case is used to denote the class that constitutes the basis of comparison:

> *Seneca erat sapientissimus Romanorum.*
> Seneca was the wisest of the Romans.

5.7 PLACE/LOCATION EXPRESSIONS

English and Latin both rely heavily on prepositional phrases to indicate place where, place to which, and place from which. The most common anomaly in English is offered by the word 'home'; contrast:

> We're heading to Ohio.

> We're heading to the market.

> We're heading to the house.

> We're heading home.

The most common anomalies in Latin are offered by the names of cities, towns, and small islands and by the nouns *domus, humus,* and *rus.* All of these words express place where (i.e., place in or at which) by means of the locative (see §4.3.7), a vestigial Indo-European case. Otherwise, with all other nouns, the preposition *in* with the ablative is used to express place at which or place in which:

> *in oppido:* at/in the town
>
> *in villa:* at/in the house
>
> *in foro:* at/in the forum

Again, with the names of cities, towns, and small islands and the nouns *domus, humus,* and *rus,* place from which is expressed without a preposition by the ablative case:

> *Roma veniunt:* They are coming from Rome.
>
> *domo veniunt:* They are coming from home.

Otherwise, with all other nouns, the prepositions *a/ab, de,* and *e/ex* with the ablative are used to express place from which:

> *ab oppido veniunt:* They are coming from town.
>
> *e villa veniunt:* They are coming out of the house.
>
> *de foro veniunt:* They are coming down from the forum.

And once again, with the names of cities, towns, and small islands and the nouns *domus, humus,* and *rus,* place to which is expressed without a preposition by the accusative case:

> *Romam veniunt:* They are coming to Rome.
>
> *domum veniunt:* They are coming home.

Otherwise, with all other nouns, the prepositions *ad* and *in* with the accusative are used to express place to which:

> *ad oppidum veniunt:* They are coming to town.
>
> *in villam veniunt:* They are coming into the house.
>
> *in forum veniunt:* They are coming into the forum.

Finally, with the names of cities, towns, and small islands and the nouns *domus, humus,* and *rus,* the use of prepositions indicates approximation:

in Roma sunt: They are in the area of Rome.

a Roma veniunt: They are coming from the vicinity of Rome.

ad Romam veniunt: They are coming toward the direction of Rome.

5.8 DESCRIPTION

In English, descriptions much depend on the prepositions 'of' and 'with', as you can see from the translations that follow.

In Latin, fairly subtle distinctions are drawn: whether the object described is animate or not and whether the quality described is abstract or concrete.

If something animate is being described and it's an abstract quality, the genitive of description is employed:

femina sapientiae notae: a woman of famous wisdom

If something animate is being described and it's a concrete quality, the ablative of description is employed:

femina longis digitis: a woman with long fingers

When something inanimate is described in terms of its material, either a genitive of material or an ablative of material is used (with a preposition *de* or *e/ex,* or optionally without a preposition but with a modifier):

statua auri: a statue of gold

statua (ex) auro pretioso: a statue of expensive gold

And when something inanimate is described in terms of an abstract quality, again a genitive of description will be used:

statua magnae artis: a statue of great art

6. ADJECTIVES

An **adjective** is a word that characterizes or describes a noun. In English, adjectives are most commonly placed directly before the noun that they modify and after the article, if there is one.

The <u>wise</u> father praises a <u>good</u> son.

Exceptions to this rule include poetic expression,

Once upon a midnight <u>dreary</u>. . . .

and certain common adjectival phrases derived from French (e.g., 'a court martial', 'an heir apparent', 'an attorney general') as well as adjectives expanded to form adjectival phrases, particularly participles:

The <u>happy</u> <u>child</u> squealed with delight.

<u>Happy</u> with his new toy, the <u>child</u> squealed with delight.

The <u>defeated</u> <u>sailors</u> collected their dead.

<u>Defeated</u> by the Romans, the <u>sailors</u> collected their dead.

We must save the <u>drowning</u> <u>men</u>.

We must save the <u>men</u> <u>drowning</u> in the sea.

In all instances, however, word order is the mechanism through which the language makes clear which noun is being modified by which adjective—in most cases, the closest one. Failure to observe this rule results in such grammatical irregularities as the so-called misplaced modifier:

Drowning in the sea, the captain ordered the men to be rescued.

English adjectives (with the exception of the demonstratives 'this' and 'that') lack the distinction of singular and plural forms that the nouns possess:

The <u>young</u> girl attracted the attention of the <u>young</u> boys.

Latin adjectives, like its nouns, are declined. They, in fact, fall into three of the same declensional classes as the nouns, with the same endings. The difference is that each noun typically has a unique gender and therefore has a single set of singular and plural endings. An adjective itself has no intrinsic gender but rather has different sets of forms for different genders (either all three or just two, in certain adjectives where masculine and feminine have the same endings; some 3rd-declension adjectives have only one ending for the masculine, feminine, and neuter in the nominative singular).

These multiple forms are necessitated by the **rule of agreement**: an adjective must be in the same gender, case, and number as the noun it modifies:

vir fortis: strong man

omnes urbes: all cities

nave celeri: with a swift ship

sociorum fugientium: of fleeing allies

You should bear three things in mind:

(1) The adjective and noun may not be in the same declension—for example, a 3rd-declension adjective may modify a 2nd-declension noun. In this situation (as in two of the examples above), the endings on the noun and adjective may not be the same, although they are in the same case and number.

(2) Latin does not share the English language's capacity to use nouns as adjectives, for example, 'house guest' or 'wine bottle'. Seemingly equivalent Latin expressions like *verbivelitatio* 'word skirmish' and *viocurus* 'road curator' are really single, compound nouns, as indicated by the fact that only the second element is declined. However, several compound words in Latin, like *respublica* 'commonwealth' and *ususfructus* 'the right of usufruct', do exhibit declension in both elements, and some editors therefore elect to print them as two separate words.

(3) You will notice that Latin often uses an adjective where in English an adverb would be expected:

Caesar imprudens hostibus credidit: Caesar <u>imprudently</u> trusted his enemies.

6.1 ATTRIBUTIVE AND PREDICATIVE POSITION

In Latin noun phrases, an adjective that expresses number, size, or quantity is typically placed before the noun, as is the standard case in English; other descriptive adjectives are usually found after the noun. The foregoing observation is to be suspended in poetry, where Latin word order enjoys much greater freedom and adjectives are very commonly separated from their nouns by at least one other word. Adjective strings usually don't use conjunctions for separation; the only notable exception is *multus, -a, -um,* which may or may not employ a conjunction.

> *viri boni nobiles:* good and noble men
>
> *multi (et) ingentes viri:* many enormous men

This is called the **attributive use** of the adjective. In English, the **predicative use** of the adjective requires a verb, which is also a common construction in Latin:

> The man is good.
>
> *vir est bonus.*

There is also the less common possibility, however, of omitting forms of the verb 'to be' in such sentences. This use of the adjective alone as a complete predicate is most often signaled by its placement in an unusual position:

> *viri ingentes:* The men are huge.
>
> *boni viri:* The men are good.

6.2 DEGREES OF COMPARISON

The adjectives discussed thus far are said to be in the **positive** degree:

> The teacher is <u>wise</u>.

> The Romans are <u>courageous</u>.

In the expression of a comparison, the **comparative** degree of the adjective is employed:

> The teacher is wis<u>er</u> than the student.

> The Romans are <u>more</u> courageous than the Parthians.

The **superlative** degree indicates the highest level of the quality in question:

Seneca is the wis<u>est</u> teacher.

The Romans are the <u>most</u> courageous of the Italians.

As these examples show, English forms the comparative degree by adding the suffix -*er* to short adjectives (generally either monosyllabic or disyllabic and ending in -*y*) and using the adverb 'more' with all others. Similarly, the superlative is formed by adding the suffix -*est* to shorter adjectives and using the adverb 'most' with all others.

These same three degrees of adjectives are found in Latin. The positive degree is the dictionary entry form of the adjective:

magister est sapien<u>s</u>.

Romani sunt fort<u>es</u>.

Like English, Latin forms the comparative degree by adding a suffix to the adjectival stem:

magister est sapient<u>ior</u> quam discipulus.

Romani sunt fort<u>iores</u> Parthis.

Similarly for the superlative degree:

Seneca est magister sapient<u>issimus</u>.

Romani sunt fort<u>issimi</u> Italicorum.

The semantic range of the Latin comparative and superlative forms is somewhat broader than that of the English. In addition to meaning strictly 'more', the Latin comparative can also mean 'rather' or 'excessively'. The superlative can mean simply 'very' or 'exceedingly', without necessarily implying absolutely the most.

6.2.1 Irregular Comparisons: Like English, Latin has a small number of adjectives whose comparative and superlative degrees are irregularly built on different stems. These are among the most common of adjectives, and you will encounter them often:

good: *bonus, melior, optimus*

bad: *malus, peior, pessimus*

large: *magnus, maior, maximus*

small: *parvus, minor, minimus*

much: *multus, plus, plurimus*

many: *multi, plures, plurimi*

Less common, especially in the positive degree, but still notable are the following:

outward: *exterus, exterior, extremus*

below: *inferus, inferior, infimus* or *imus*

worthless: *nequam, nequior, nequissimus*

following: *posterus, posterior, postremus*

above: *superus, superior, supremus* or *summus*

Some adjectives lack a positive degree, being found only in the comparative and superlative:

nearer, nearest: *citerior, citimus*

worse, worst: *deterior, deterrimus*

inner, inmost: *interior, intimus*

former, first: *prior, primus*

closer, closest: *propior, proximus*

farther, farthest: *ulterior, ultimus*

6.3 DEMONSTRATIVE ADJECTIVES

Latin demonstrative adjectives such as *hic* 'this' and *ille* 'that' are similar in use and meaning to their English equivalents. Moreover, they more often precede their noun, especially in prose:

hic vir: this man

or

illa femina: that woman

The **determinative** *is, ea, id* can be used as a weak demonstrative to mean either 'this' or 'that':

> *id templum:* this temple, that temple

Like any other adjective, demonstratives must agree with their nouns in gender, case, and number.

6.4 INTERROGATIVE ADJECTIVES

In English, the interrogative pronouns include 'who?' (personal) and 'what?' (impersonal). Interrogative adjectives are slightly different:

Who wrote this?	vs.	What (or Which) poet wrote this?
What did you write?	vs.	What (or Which) poem did you write?

In Latin, the forms of the interrogative adjective are identical to those of the relative pronoun:

quis hoc scripsit?	vs.	*qui poeta hoc scripsit?*
quid scripsisti?	vs.	*quod carmen scripsisti?*

6.5 POSSESSIVE ADJECTIVES

Possession is most commonly indicated in English by the possessive adjectives, which are always used without an article:

> <u>My</u> son loves <u>your</u> daughter.

> The Romans heard <u>his</u> speech with pleasure.

Alternatively, but less idiomatically, the possessive adjective can be replaced by a genitival prepositional phrase:

> A son <u>of mine</u> loves that daughter <u>of yours</u>.

> The Romans heard that speech <u>of his</u> with great enjoyment.

For the 1st and 2nd persons and for the 3rd-person reflexive, Latin has the possessive adjectives *meus, tuus,* and *suus* in the singular and *noster, vester,* and *suus* in the plural. They usually follow their nouns:

filius meus filiam tuam amat.

Much less commonly than English, however, Latin may instead employ the genitive of the personal pronoun:

filius mei filiam tui amat.

This pronominal construction is always used (in Latin) for the 3rd person (non-reflexive) possessive:

Romani orationem <u>eius</u> magno cum gaudio audiebant.

6.6 INTENSIVE ADJECTIVE

The **intensive adjective** in English is distinctive in that, like the demonstratives and unlike other adjectives, it uses a distinctive form for the plural:

himself, herself, itself → themselves

The English intensive must be clearly differentiated from the English reflexive pronoun (see §8.2):

He himself killed. [INTENSIVE]

He killed himself. [REFLEXIVE][1]

The Latin intensive, *ipse, ipsa, ipsum,* is fairly straightforward. In the nominative, it sometimes precedes its noun, but in the oblique cases it usually follows:

ipse Caesar: Caesar <u>himself</u>

feminas ipsas: the women <u>themselves</u>

---

1. Another usage to be noted in English is with the preposition 'by' to mean 'alone' or 'without others':

He killed by himself.

6.7 ADJECTIVES USED SUBSTANTIVELY

In English, we frequently use adjectives as nouns, often by simply adding the definite article before them. The adjectives typically refer to indefinite plural people or things or else to an antecedent already expressed:

> The land of the free [people] and the home of the brave [people]. . . .

> When it comes to dinner, I prefer the quick and easy [things].

> I wear a large sweater; don't give me the medium [sweater].

Latin can use adjectives in essentially the same ways (except without a definite article):

> *omnes erant laeti:* All [people] were happy.

> *sunt pauperibus pauca:* The poor [people] have few [things].

> *filiae meae sunt pulchrae, sed maior est etiam callida:* My daughters are lovely, but the elder [daughter] is also clever.

A singular adjective used substantively (i.e., as a noun) is commonly employed in Latin for generalizations:

> *sapiens nihil metuit:* The wise [person] fears nothing.

7. ARTICLES

In English, the definite article is used with a noun when it is being discussed as a specific entity:

We always honor the gods.

The indefinite article, which typically only occurs in the singular, marks a noun as a member of a class, without specifying which member:

A god will punish the evil tyrant.

Plural nouns may be used with no article, to indicate generic groups in general statements:

Gods are more powerful than mortals.

Latin, however, has no definite article, and it has no indefinite article:

deus: a god, the god, god

Occasionally this ambiguity can be a bit difficult for Latin students, especially early on. Context, though, will clear up most ambiguities and will guide you toward the best translation. It may be added here that the ancient Romans appear not to have been much troubled by their lack of articles.[1]

---

1. Interestingly, the Romance languages (i.e., the languages derived from Latin) did develop a definite article (usually evolved from the Latin *ille, illa, illud*) and an indefinite article (usually evolved from the Latin number *unus, una, unum*).

8. PRONOUNS I

The usage of pronouns, as we saw defined in §2, is fairly straightforward: pronouns are used in place of nouns. Their variety in number, their paradigms, and their semantic complexity in both English and Latin, however, can make pronouns a challenging bit of learning. In this chapter, we'll examine the most common Latin pronouns (and their English counterparts), reserving less frequent pronominal expressions for the next chapter.

All Latin pronouns exhibit the features of number and case, although not all pronouns are found in all cases. As for the feature of gender, all pronouns do exhibit gender with the exception of 1st- and 2nd-person pronouns and the reflexive pronoun. Not all pronouns differentiate all three genders (e.g., masculine and feminine merge in indefinite and interrogative pronouns).

Many pronouns are actually derived from related adjectives; as such, they tend to have familiar declensions (though they may exhibit anomalies in the genitive and dative singular and/or in the neuter nominative/accusative singular). True pronouns tend to have irregular declensions and must, therefore, be learned thoroughly.

8.1 PERSONAL PRONOUNS (SEE §2.4)

In English, the 1st-person pronouns are, in the singular, 'I' (subjective), 'me' (objective), and 'mine' (possessive); and in the plural, 'we' (subjective), 'us' (objective), and 'ours' (possessive).

I think Seneca will welcome us.

This shop is mine, but we can buy another.

The 2nd-person pronouns in English are 'you' (subjective and objective) and 'yours' (possessive). Standard modern English doesn't distinguish between singular and plural in the 2nd person, sometime creating an ambiguity:

You, Nero, think Seneca will welcome you.
(In this sentence, is the 'you' doing the thinking, Nero, synonymous with the 'you' Seneca will welcome? Perhaps Seneca will welcome Nero and Agrippina. It's impossible to know without more context or greater specificity—hence the ambiguity.)

This shop is <u>yours</u>, but <u>you</u> can buy others.

(Is this shop owned by one 'you' or multiple 'yous'? Will the future shops be purchased by a singular 'you' or a plural 'you'?)

Latin doesn't have this ambiguity because it distinguishes clearly between the 2nd singular and 2nd plural pronouns.

The 3rd-person pronoun in English distinguishes between gender in the singular: 'he', 'she', and 'it' (subjective); 'him', 'her', and 'it' (objective); and 'his', 'hers', and 'its' (possessive). This distinction isn't preserved in the plural, however: 'they' (subjective), 'them' (objective), and 'theirs' (possessive) are used for all three genders.

The books, which were <u>theirs</u>, <u>they</u> handed over to <u>them</u>.

In Latin, the 1st-person pronoun and the 2nd-person pronoun have rather irregular declensions in the singular, but they're usually easy enough to identify. The 3rd-person pronoun in Latin is somewhat complicated in its choices; the determinative pronoun (*is, ea, id*) is the most common choice; two of the demonstrative adjectives (*hic, haec, hoc* and *ille, illa, illud*) are also often used without substantives and function as 3rd-person pronouns.

As noted above, like English, Latin does not distinguish gender with 1st- and 2nd-person pronouns—that distinction only occurs with the 3rd-person pronoun (in English, only in the singular of the 3rd-person pronoun).

In Latin, more than English, the so-called plural of majesty (aka "royal plural" or "nosism") occurs with the 1st-person pronoun. This usage is most common in self-reference by a poet.

nos laudant.
They praise <u>us</u> [i.e., <u>me</u>].

te laudamus.
<u>We</u> [i.e., <u>I</u>] praise you.

Like English, Latin can employ the 2nd-person pronoun impersonally for imaginary persons:

tu esse sapiens debes: You [i.e., a person] ought to be wise.

(Latin could also express this idea with a 3rd-person indefinite or distributive construction: *quisque esto sapiens:* Let every/each [person] be wise!)

Finally, the emphatic forms for the 1st and 2nd pronouns are: *egomet* and *nosmet* and *tute* and *vosmet* in the nominative; *mihimet* and *nobismet* and *tibimet* and *vobismet* in the dative; *meme* and *nosmet* and *tete* and *vosmet* in the accusative; and *meme* and *nobismet* and *tete* and *vobismet* in the ablative. For the genitive, there are no emphatics in either the singular or the plural.

8.2 REFLEXIVE PRONOUNS

Since they refer back to the subject of their clause or sentence, **reflexive pronouns** can occur only in the oblique cases in the predicate.

First-person reflexive: This is simply a form of the 1st-person pronoun; the intensive pronoun in the nominative can also be used for emphasis.

> *mihi nocui:* I hurt myself.

> *ipse mihi nocui:* I hurt myself.

Second-person reflexive: This behaves just like the 1st-person pronoun.

> *vobis nocuistis:* You hurt yourselves.

> *ipsae vobis nocuistis:* You hurt yourselves.

Third-person reflexive: in both the singular and plural, regardless of gender, occurring only in the oblique cases, there are *sui, sibi, se(se), se(se)*. Again, emphasis on the reflexivity is conveyed with a nominative use of the intensive.

> *sibi nocuerunt:* They hurt themselves.

> *ipsi sibi nocuerunt:* They hurt themselves.[1]

---

1. We should be alert to the different ways we use the -self pronoun in English. It can be reflexive (I hurt myself); it can be intensive (I myself was hurt); or with the preposition 'by' it can communicate isolation (I went off by myself). Three different pronouns or adjectives will convey these three different ideas in Latin.

8.3 DEMONSTRATIVE PRONOUNS

The most common demonstratives in Latin are offered by forms of *ille, illa, illud* (that) and *hic, haec, hoc* (this).

> *haec quam illa malumus.*
> We prefer these [things] to those [things].

Nearly as common is the pronoun *iste, ista, istud* (that of yours [singular or plural]); this pronoun is often used pejoratively.

> *ista faciebamus.*
> We were doing those [darned] things of yours.

The determinative *is, ea, id* can function as a weak demonstrative:

> *ea malumus:* We prefer these/those [things].

Another determinative, a compound of *is, ea, id*, the pronoun *idem, eadem, idem* (which, again, can also function as an adjective) means 'the same' or 'the very same':

> *eidem dixerunt:* The very same [people] spoke.

8.4 RELATIVE PRONOUNS (SEE §2.4)

Keep in mind that besides serving as pronouns, **relative pronouns** also have the syntactical function of a subordinating conjunction (see §§19 and 28.2).

We can't trust that man who talks of peace but prepares for war.

The relative pronoun here introduces the subordinate clause ("talks of peace but prepares for war").

In English, the relative pronouns 'who', 'whom', 'which', 'whose', and 'that' do not distinguish between singular and plural. 'Who', 'whom', and 'whose' are masculine or feminine; 'which' is typically neuter; 'that' can be used for any gender; and 'whose' can be used for neuters where 'of which' sounds awkward. Finally, in terms of proper case, 'who', 'which', and 'that' are subjective case; 'whose', 'that's', and, less commonly, 'of which' are possessive; and 'whom', 'which', and 'that' are objective.

Latin employs an array of different relatives. When translating the Latin relative into English, you must take great care with the proper choice of 'who', 'whom', 'which', 'whose', and 'of which'.

The **simple relative** pronoun is *qui, quae, quod,* which closely resembles the interrogative pronoun in much of its declension.

> *vir qui Caesarem admirabatur mortuus est.*
> The man who admired Caesar died.

> *vir quem Caesar admirabatur mortuus est.*
> The man whom Caesar admired died.

For the syntactical rules governing the use of relative pronouns within independent and dependent clauses, see §19.

8.5 INTERROGATIVE PRONOUNS

The interrogative pronoun in English closely resembles the relative pronoun in form, except that 'that' isn't used, while 'what' (neuter, singular, subjective, or objective) is. In terms of usage, interrogative pronouns are used to ask direct questions and indirect questions:

> Who are you?

> Whom do they seek?

> Whose poem were you listening to?

> I ask who you are.

> I ask whom they seek.

> I ask whose poem you were listening to.

The **simple interrogative** pronoun in Latin (*quis, quid*) can be distinguished from the simple relative in that the former is more often used in the singular and in that the masculine and feminine genders are not differentiated.

> *quis es?*
> Who [potentially masculine or feminine] are you?

quem petunt?

Whom [potentially masculine or feminine; potentially singular or plural] do they seek?[2]

cuius carmen audiebatis?

Whose [potentially masculine or feminine] poem were you listening to?

8.6 INDEFINITE PRONOUNS

In English, the **indefinite pronouns** are 'some', 'any', 'a certain [one]', 'someone', 'somebody', 'something', 'anyone', 'anybody', and 'anything'.

'Any' and its compounds are true indefinites in that they refer to persons or things unknown. 'Some' and its compounds and 'a certain [one]' can refer to persons or things whose actual identities are known but not specified or disclosed.

English also has the **emphatic indefinites**: 'no matter who/whom/whose/what/which'; 'whoever', 'whomever', 'whosever', 'whatever', 'whichever'; and 'whosoever', 'whomsoever', 'whatsoever'.

As for Latin, the **simple indefinite pronoun** *aliquis, aliquid,* built from the interrogative plus the prefix *ali-,* refers to person(s) or thing(s) unknown; the pronoun may be declined in the plural.[3] The pronoun *quidam, quaedam, quiddam,* built mostly on the relative pronoun plus the suffix *-dam,* refers to person(s) or thing(s) whose actual identities are known but not specified or disclosed; again, this pronoun may be declined in the plural.

cognoscisne aliquem?

Do you recognize anyone?

---

2. While the plural *quos petunt?* is grammatically acceptable, it communicates that the speaker wants to know the specific names or identities of the (plural) persons being sought. That is, the answer to *quem petunt?* could properly be *senatores* 'senators', but the proper answer to a question like *quos petunt?* would have to be something like *C. Cassium et M. Brutum* 'Gaius Cassius and Marcus Brutus'.

3. For this pronoun and the many adverbs sharing the *ali-* prefix, remember this little ditty: "After *si, nisi, num,* and *ne,* all the *ali*-s drop away"; to this list of conjunctions should be added *neu* and *neve.*

cognoscisne quendam?
> Do you recognize a certain someone?

The pronouns *nonnullus, nonnulla, nonnullum* 'some [i.e., not none]' and *ullus, ulla, ullum* 'any' can also serve as indefinites:

habesne ulla?
> Have you any [things]?

nonnulla habemus.
> We have some.

Negative indefinite pronouns: This duty is carried by the irregular nouns *nemo* 'no one' and *nihil* 'nothing' and even the noun phrase *nulla res* 'no thing'; occasionally *nullus, nulla, nullum* is used as a pronoun (especially in the genitive and ablative cases):

cognoscisne neminem?
> Do you recognize no one?

cognoscisne nihil?
> Do you recognize nothing?

eum nullius rei pudet.
> He is ashamed of nothing.

servi a nullo empti sunt.
> The slaves were bought by no one.

When the ambient grammar dictates the use of the negating conjunction *ne* where *aliquis* would be used, the resulting negative indefinite is often written as a single word: *nequis, nequid.*

discessit necui [= ne alicui] noceret.
> He left so not to harm anyone.

Latin's **emphatic indefinites** are *quivis, quaevis, quidvis* and *quilibet, quaelibet, quidlibet*, meaning 'any whatsoever', 'anyone you please', 'anything you please'.

quaelibet uxor bona fiet.
> Anyone whatsoever will make a good wife.

elige quidvis!
> Pick anything you please!

Slightly less emphatic than the previous two is the pronoun *quispiam, quidpiam* 'any at all', 'some at all'.

> *quempiam non videbimus.*
> We will not see <u>anybody at all</u>.

8.7 POSSESSIVE PRONOUNS

In Latin, the genitives of the 1st and 2nd personal and reflexive pronouns only very rarely serve as the possessive pronouns; the preferred alternative is the use of the possessive and reflexive adjectives (based on the personal pronouns; see §6.5). The genitives of demonstrative pronouns, on the other hand, are regularly used to express possession.

> *filia eius:* his daughter
>
> *equites horum:* their cavalry

8.8 INTENSIVE PRONOUN

The Latin pronoun *ipse, ipsa, ipsum*, which can also function as an intensive adjective (see §6.6), means 'himself', 'herself', 'itself', or 'themselves'.

> *ipse dixit:* He <u>himself</u> has spoken.

The following chart will help systematize some of the information from this chapter:

PERSONAL PRONOUNS

	1st Person	2nd Person	3rd Person
SIMPLE	*ego/nos*, etc.	*tu/vos*, etc.	*is, ea, id*, etc. *hic, haec, hoc*, etc. *ille, illa, illud*, etc.
EMPHATIC/ INTENSIVE	with suffixes *-me* or *-met*	with suffixes *-te* or *-met*	*ipse* with simple [or see §9.1.1]
	ipse with simple	*ipse* with simple	
REFLEXIVE	*me/nos*, etc.	*te/vos*, etc.	*se(se)/se(se)*, etc.
POSSESSIVE	[uses possessive adjective]	[uses possessive adjective]	*eius/eorum*, etc. *huius/horum*, etc. *illius/illorum*, etc.

9. PRONOUNS II

In the previous chapter, we surveyed the most common Latin pronouns, establishing most of the pronoun types and many of their varieties. In the present chapter, we examine the remaining types and varieties.

9.1 DEMONSTRATIVE PRONOUNS (SEE §8.3)

9.1.1 Deictic: The **deictic**[1] suffix *-ce* can be added to some forms of the demonstrative pronouns *hic, haec, hoc* and *ille, illa, illud* and *iste, ista, istud* for emphasis:

> *hosce:* these ones <u>here</u>
>> *hosce cepimus.*
>> We captured these ones <u>here</u>.

> *illisce:* with those [things] <u>there</u>
>> *id illisce fecimus.*
>> We did it with those [things] <u>there</u>.

When the demonstrative ends in a vowel or an *-m*, the final *-e* of the *-ce* deictic suffix is typically omitted:

> [*horumce*] → [*horunce*] → *horunc:* of these <u>here</u>
>> *domus horunc captae sunt.*
>> The homes of these <u>here</u> were captured.

> *illaec:* those [women] *there*
>> *illaec sunt potentissimae.*
>> Those [women] <u>there</u> are very powerful.

> *cum istoc:* with that [one] <u>there</u> of yours
>> *cum istoc apparuerunt.*
>> They appeared with that [one] <u>there</u> of yours.

---

1. **Deictic**, from the Greek verb 'to show', means directly pointing out or indicating, as if one is pointing a linguistic finger at a person or object.

9.1.2 Quantitative: Latin also has the **quantitative demonstrative** *tantus, -a, -um* (which is actually an adjective commonly used substantively) meaning 'so great', 'so much'.

nemo ferre tanta potest.
No one can endure <u>such great</u> [things].

villas tanti numquam videramus.
We had never seen villas worth <u>so much</u>.

9.1.3 Qualitative: Finally, there is a **qualitative demonstrative** *talis, -e* (again, derived from an adjective) meaning 'such', 'of such a type', 'of such a sort'.

nemo ferre talia potest.
No one can endure <u>things of such a type</u>.

talibus numquam occurreramus.
We had never encountered <u>such</u> [people].

9.2 RELATIVE PRONOUNS (SEE §8.4)

9.2.1 Indefinite/General: Consider the **indefinite relatives** (also called the **general relatives**) *quicumque, quaecumque, quodcumque* and *quisquis, quaequae, quicquid,* both of which mean 'whoever', 'whatever', 'whosoever', 'whatsoever', 'anyone who', 'anything which', and so on. The former pronoun is just a compound of the simple relative (§8.4) plus the undeclined (and separable) suffix *-cumque;* the latter is a doubling of the simple interrogative pronoun (§8.5), in which both elements are declined:

senatus quemcumque populus honestat.
The senate pays honor to <u>anyone</u> the populace does.

Parthi illis pepercerunt quiqui se tradiderunt.
The Parthians spared those <u>whosoever</u> surrendered.

9.2.2 Qualitative: Latin's **qualitative relative** pronouns, based on adjectives, are *qualis, quale* 'such as', 'of such a sort as', and its compounds *qualiscumque, qualecumque* and *qualisqualis, qualequale,* both meaning 'of whatever sort/quality/kind'.

> *Scipio viros numquam laudavit quales Hannibal laudare solet.*
> Scipio has never praised men <u>such as</u> Hannibal is accustomed to.

> *Caesar equos habere potest qualescumque cupit.*
> Caesar can have <u>whatever sorts of</u> horses he desires.

9.2.3 Quantitative: And finally, Latin employs the **quantitative relative** pronouns *quantus, quantum* 'as great as' and *quot* (indeclinable) 'as many as'.

> *Caesar hos equos non pendet quanti fiunt.*
> Caesar won't value these horses, <u>as big as</u> they become.

9.3 INTERROGATIVE PRONOUNS (SEE §8.5)

9.3.1 Quantitative: The **quantitative interrogatives,** based on adjectives, are *quantus, quantum* 'how big?', *quot* (indeclinable) 'how many?', and *quotus, quotum* 'of what number?'.

> *pro quotis orationem habuit?*
> In front of <u>how many</u> did he speak?

> *quantum erat vincere Parthios?*
> <u>How big</u> [a thing] was it to defeat the Parthians?

9.3.2 Qualitative: The **qualitative interrogative,** also based on an adjective, is *qualis, quale* 'what sort of?', 'of what kind?'.

> *qualia possumus ferre?*
> <u>What</u> [kind of things] can we endure?

> *quales vidistis?*
> <u>What sort</u> [of people] did you see?

9.3.3 Emphatic: The **emphatic interrogative**, again based on an adjective, is *quisnam, quidnam* 'who indeed?', 'what indeed?'.

> *quisnam loqui audet?*
> <u>Who indeed</u> dares to speak?

9.3.4 Indefinite: One **indefinite interrogative** in Latin is *ecquis, ecquae, ecquid*, 'anyone', 'anything', 'someone', 'something'.

> *ecquid vis?*
> Do you want <u>anything</u>/<u>something</u>?

Somewhat more emphatic than this is the pronoun *numquis, numquid*.

> *numquid vis?*
> Is there <u>any</u>thing/<u>some</u>thing you want?

9.4 INDEFINITE PRONOUNS (SEE §8.6)

9.4.1 Generalizing: English's most common **generalizing indefinite pronouns** are 'everyone', 'everybody', 'everything', 'each', and 'all'.

Latin's **generalizing indefinite** pronoun, *omnis, omne* 'all', 'entire', 'every', is based on the adjective *omnis, omne*.

> *omnes Senecam male ferunt.*
> <u>All</u> [people] are annoyed by Seneca.[2]

Besides *omnis, omne*, Latin's most common generalizing pronoun is *quisque, quaeque, quodque* 'each':

> *cuique dedimus:* We gave <u>to each</u>, <u>to everybody</u>.

> *quisque erat liber:* <u>Each</u>/<u>everyone</u>/<u>everybody</u> was free.

Also to be found are *unusquisque, unaquaeque, unumquidque* (sometimes printed as two separate words) 'each individually' and *uterque, utraque, utrumque* 'each of two'.

---

2. Made definite with the addition of a genitive:
   omnes <u>Romanorum</u> Senecam male ferunt.
   All <u>of the Romans</u> are annoyed by Seneca.

9.5 COMPARATIVE PRONOUNS

Comparative pronouns are exclusively used when two persons or objects are referred to. The Latin ones found here, all derived from adjectives, have no simple counterparts in English.

9.5.1 Demonstrative: The **comparative demonstrative** pronouns are *alter, altera, alterum* 'the other of two' and *neuter, neutra, neutrum* 'neither of two'.

> *elige alterum.*
> Choose the other one.

> *elige neutrum.*
> Choose neither.

9.5.2 Interrogative: The **comparative interrogative** pronoun is *uter, utra, utrum* 'which of two?'.

> *utrum elegit?*
> Which [of the two] did he choose?

9.5.3 Relative: The **comparative relative** pronoun *utercumque, utracumque, utrumcumque* 'whichever of two' is used in Latin.

> *elige utrumcumque tibi placet.*
> Choose whichever [of the two] pleases you.

9.5.4 Indefinite: Lastly, we come to the Latin **comparative indefinite** pronouns: *utercumque, utracumque, utrumcumque* 'whichever of the two', 'some(one) of two' is the most common.

> *elige utrumcumque*
> Choose whichever [of the two].

Also to be found are the compounds *uterlibet, utralibet, utrumlibet* and *utervis, utravis, utrumvis* 'whichever of two' and *alteruter, alterautra, alterumutrum* (sometimes printed as two separate words) 'one or the other of two'.

9.6 PARTICULARIZING PRONOUNS

Particularizing pronouns in English run a wide gamut: 'each', 'either', 'neither', 'both', 'the other', 'the only', 'none'. Unlike Latin, English doesn't always distinguish with its pronouns between duals and plurals: 'each of two' or 'each of several', 'the other of two' or 'the other of several', 'the only of two' or 'the only of several'. But sometimes it does: 'either [of two]', 'neither [of two]', 'both [of two]', 'none [of several]'.

Latin offers a number of common particularizing pronouns, all derived from adjectives, for example,

alius, alia, aliud: 'the other of several'

alter, altera, alterum: 'the other of two'

unusquisque, unaquaeque, unumquidque (sometimes printed as two separate words): 'each individually' (see §9.4)

uterque, utraque, utrumque: 'each of two' (see §9.4)

solus, sola, solum: 'the only', 'the sole', 'the one alone'

neuter, neutra, neutrum: 'neither of two' (see §9.5.1)

ceterus, cetera, ceterum: 'the other', 'the rest'

9.6.1 Indefinite: Latin's simple indefinite pronoun, *aliquis, aliquid,* also serves as one of its **indefinite particularizing** pronouns 'another', 'an [indefinite] other', 'some other', and is based on the indefinite adjective *aliquis, aliqua, aliquid.*

> *hoc est nequam; da mihi aliquid.*
> This is worthless; give me <u>some other</u>.

Quisquam, quaequam, quidquam is used with negation and with slight emphasis to mean 'not a single one'.

> *in illa terra ne quisquam quidem nos cognovit.*
> In that land <u>not even a single person</u> recognized us.

The compound *nescioquis, nescioquid* (sometimes printed as two separate words) literally means 'I don't know who' or 'I don't know what' but in usage commonly means 'someone or other' or 'something or other'.

> *nescioquis loquebatur.*
> <u>Someone or other</u> was speaking

9.7 RECIPROCAL PRONOUNS

The Latin **reciprocal pronouns** (*alii, aliae, alia* and *alter, altera, alterum*) are used twice in the same clause, the first time usually in the nominative and in an oblique case the second time:

> *alii alios viderunt.*
> They all saw <u>each other</u>
>
> *alter alterum vidit.*
> The two of them saw <u>each other</u>.

9.8 INDIRECT REFLEXIVE PRONOUNS

We saw above in §8.2 that a reflexive is used in the predicate to refer back to the subject of its clause or sentence. But in a complex sentence, in its subordinate clause, a reflexive pronoun can be used in two different ways. First, it can refer back to the subject of its own clause, in which case it is a so-called **direct reflexive**.

> She urges them to free <u>themselves</u>. [i.e., she urges them, "Free yourselves!"]
> *hortatur eos ut se liberent.*

Or, second, it can refer back to the subject of the main clause, *but only if the subordinate clause assumes the thoughts, words, or intentions of the main clause's subject.*[3]

> She urges them to free <u>her</u>. [i.e., she urges them, "Free me!"]
>
> *hortatur eos ut se liberent.*

This use of the pronoun is called the **indirect reflexive**. Because even some native Latin speakers found this distinction confusing, the pronoun *ipse, ipsa, ipsum* (and less often *is, ea, id*) can be observed in use instead of the indirect reflexive.

> She urges them to free her.
>
> *hortatur eos ut ipsam liberent.*

To be sure, the extensive battery of Latin pronouns can seem a bit overwhelming. It may be useful to visualize this pronominal system as a spectrum; the categories differentiated above simply name the primary colors; each individual pronoun represents a particular hue that blends and blurs into the pronouns that are semantically closest to it. This subtle "coloration" exhibited by the pronominal system provides us with a great insight into one of the niceties of the Latin language.

The following chart will help systematize most of the information from this chapter and some of the information from the previous chapter:

---

3. If it doesn't, some other pronoun (demonstrative or determinative) is used.

> She urges them to free <u>these</u> [people].
>
> *hortatur eos ut <u>hos</u> liberent.*

	DEMONSTRATIVE	RELATIVE	INDEFINITE	INTERROGATIVE
SIMPLE	*is, ea, id* *hic, haec, hoc* *ille, illa, illud* *iste, ista, istud* *idem, eadem, idem*	*qui, quae, quod*	*aliquis, aliquid* *quidam, quaedam, quiddam* *nonnullus, etc.* *ullus, ulla, ullum*	*quis, quid*
negative			[*nemo, nihil, nulla res*] *nullus, nulla, nullum* *nequis, nequid*	
EMPHATIC/ INTENSIVE	*ipse, ipsa, ipsum* deictic suffix *-ce*		*quispiam, quidpiam* *quivis, quaevis, quidvis* *quilibet, etc.*	*quisnam, quidnam*
QUANTITATIVE	*tantus, tanta, tantum*	*quantus, etc.* *quot*		*quantus, quantum* *quot* *quotus, quotum*
QUALITATIVE	*talis, tale*	*qualis, quale* *qualiscumque, etc.* *qualisqualis, etc.*		*qualis, quale*
COMPARATIVE	*alter, altera, alterum*	*utercumque, etc.* *utervis, etc.* *uterlibet, etc.* *alteruter, etc.*	*utercumque, etc.*	*uter, utra, utrum*
negative	*neuter, neutra, neutrum*			
GENERALIZING	*uterque, utraque, utrumque*	*quicumque, etc.*	*quisque, quaeque, etc.* *omnis, omne* *unusquisque, etc.* *uterque, etc.*	*ecquis, ecquae, ecquid* *numquis, numquid*
PARTICULARIZING	*solus, sola, solum* *uterque, utraque, utrumque*		*aliquis, aliquid* *alius, alia, aliud* *ceterus, cetera, ceterum* *quisquam, etc.* *nescioquis, etc.*	

10. PREPOSITIONS

A preposition is a word used in a phrase with a noun (or its equivalent) expressing that noun's relationship to another word or idea. Among the more common such relationships in English are the following:

Location:	The farmer is in the field.
Direction:	The ship is sailed into the harbor.
	The thieves are running from the house.
Possession:	The words of the philosopher are wise.
Time:	We sailed for ten days.
	We arrived on the fourth day.
Agent:	This drama was written by Seneca.
Means:	They killed the wolf with stones.
Manner:	We heard the report with fear/with great fear.
Accompaniment:	I will go to the forum with my brother.

The substantive in the prepositional phrase is called the **object of the preposition**. In English, if the object is a pronoun, it will be in the objective, rather than the subjective, case:

The dog is running toward him.

This is just between you and me.

Will you come with us?

In many situations, Latin's use of the preposition is quite similar. The object of a preposition is almost always in either the ablative or the accusative case (very rarely the genitive). Some prepositions can be used with two cases, having different meanings with each case. The correct usage will be indicated as part of the dictionary entry for the preposition.

The following Latin prepositional constructions are analogous to the English examples listed above:

Location: *agricola est in agro.*

Direction: *navis in portum navigatur.*

                        fures e villa currunt.

Agent: *haec fabula a Seneca composita est.*

Manner: *cum metu nuntium audiebamus.*

Accompaniment: *ad forum cum fratre meo ibo.*

In many other situations, however, we have seen (§5) that it is the declensional ending of the noun that indicates its relationship to other parts of the sentence, thereby rendering the use of a preposition unnecessary. This is true for the remaining examples in the list above:

Possession: *verba philosophi sunt sapientia.*

Time: *decem dies navigabamus.*

                        quarta die pervenimus.

Means: *lupum saxis interfecerunt.*

Manner: *magno metu nuntium audiebamus.*

When translating such sentences from Latin into English, it will be necessary to include the appropriate English preposition, even though there is none in the Latin.

There are two things to keep in mind:

(1) The semantic ranges of seemingly equivalent prepositions in the two languages are at best overlapping, but never identical. Consider the case of the English 'with' in the examples above. When it expresses means or manner, it can be translated in Latin by a noun in the ablative case, with no preposition; when it expresses accompaniment, it is translated by the Latin preposition *cum* with the ablative case.

Particularly hazardous is the English word 'to'. It can be used to mark a noun or pronoun as an indirect object, whereas Latin simply puts the noun in the dative case:

We give gifts to the gods.

dona deis damus.

It can be used prepositionally to indicate the goal of motion.

The army was marching to the sea.

exercitus ad mare incedebat.

It is also used to form an infinitive, a grammatical form that Latin creates through inflection:

I want to see the goddess.

videre deam volo.

(2) Many verbs in English govern prepositional phrases, where the Latin equivalent takes a simple accusative direct object:

The strangers were looking at the temple.

advenae templum spectabant.

The people were listening to the speech of the praetor.

populus orationem praetoris audiebat.

When translating from English to Latin, be sure not to use a prepositional phrase with such verbs.

Occasionally words functioning as prepositions will be placed after the noun they govern. They are then said to be **postpositive**. The true prepositions *tenus* 'as far as', 'up to' and *versus* 'toward' are so used in Latin prose and others more commonly so in poetry (in a figure called **anastrophe**). When the words *causa* and *gratia* (both meaning 'on account of', 'for the sake of') function as prepositions, they are regularly postpositive.

In a poetic figure called **tmesis**, the prepositional prefix of a compound verb can occasionally be written separately from its stem. Care should be exercised here in recognizing that the nouns of the clause are *not* serving as the object of this seeming preposition.

super unus erat [= *unus supererat*]: He alone survived.

per desiderio uror [= *desiderio peruror*]: I am utterly consumed with desire.

Finally, the preposition *cum* behaves somewhat peculiarly with certain pronouns. It becomes a postpositive **enclitic** (i.e., an unaccented word attached to the word that precedes it) with all personal pronouns, the simple reflexive, the simple relative, the simple interrogative, and, by analogy, a few other simple pronouns, for example,

mecum	with me
secum	with himself/herself/themselves
quocum/quicum	with whom?
vobiscum	with you [plural]
quibuscum	with whom
utrocum	with each

III. THE SYNTAX OF VERBS AND RELATED ELEMENTS

11. VERBS

A verb is the word that expresses the acting, being, doing, and so on in a clause or sentence. Like nouns, a verb as a vocabulary item carries a semantic meaning, but it takes on a variety of different forms that indicate its precise syntactic role in the sentence or clause. Whereas a listing of all the forms of a noun is called its declension, for a verb this is called its **conjugation**, and to make such a list is to **conjugate** the verb. As was also true in the case of nouns, unfortunately not all verbs use the same set of endings. Almost all verbs belong to one of four regular conjugations, as distinguished by their consistent (or thematic) vowel(s).

Remember, verbs can be action verbs, linking verbs, or auxiliary verbs; see §2.6.

We saw that two things are needed to specify a particular noun form: case and number; for an adjective, with the addition of gender, three are required. For verbs, the number is five:

Person (three): 1st, 2nd, or 3rd

Number (two): singular or plural

Tense (six): present, future, imperfect, perfect, pluperfect, or future perfect

Voice (two): active or passive

Mood (three): indicative, imperative, or subjunctive

So, for example, the phrase "3rd-person plural pluperfect active subjunctive" will designate a unique verb form.

English verbs have one of the simplest inflectional systems of any European language. For regular verbs, the only suffixes are *-(e)s* in the present and *-(e)d* in the past. All other designations of tense, mood, or voice are formed with the auxiliary verbs: am, is, are, was, were, be, been, have, has, had, do, does, did, will, would, shall, and should. By contrast, apart from forms in the perfect passive system and periphrastic[1] (see §15), Latin never uses auxiliary verbs but rather makes all indications of person, number, tense, voice, and mood through the use of affixes, infixes, and/or stem alterations.

In English, a relatively small number of irregular verbs makes changes in the stem to form past tenses, such as know, knew, known or sink, sank, sunk. In order to use these verbs correctly in sentences, it is necessary to know all three of these forms, which are called the **principal parts** of the verb. Because they are unpredictable (if sink, sank, sunk, then why link, linked, linked and not link, lank, lunk?), they are provided by the dictionary entry for the verb and must be learned as part of English vocabulary.

The exception in English is the rule in Latin. Although there are some groups of verbs that are "regular," in the sense that knowing one form will enable you to produce all others, this is generally not the case. In Latin, it normally requires four pieces of information to generate all forms of a given verb: the present infinitive to establish which conjugation the verb conforms to, the stems to be used for the present system (i.e., the present, future, and imperfect tenses, active and passive), the perfect active system (i.e., the perfect, future perfect, and pluperfect tenses), and the perfect passive system. These are the principal parts that are provided by a Latin vocabulary or dictionary (though not all verbs have all four). The order in which these forms are listed may vary slightly in different textbooks or dictionaries, but the first will always be the same: the verb will always be listed under the 1st-person singular, present indicative form. For example, for the verb 'to send',

> *mitto, mittere, misi, missus* (or *missum*)

---

1. **Periphrasis** refers to the use of auxiliary verbs when the inflectional forms of a main verb alone just won't do. In Latin, periphrasis most often refers to future periphrastics, which are participles combined with forms of the verb 'to be'.

11.1 TRANSITIVE AND INTRANSITIVE USAGE

Verbs are classified as transitive or intransitive (a characteristic generally indicated for verbal entries in English dictionaries by the abbreviations 'tr.' or 'intr.'). A **transitive** verb is one that can govern a direct object which serves to complete its meaning:

> Everyone <u>praised</u> <u>the poet</u>.
>
> *omnes <u>poetam</u> <u>laudaverunt</u>.*

An **intransitive** verb cannot govern a direct object. The most common intransitive verb is the verb 'to be' (*sum, esse*); most verbs of motion are also intransitive:

> Vergil was a poet.
>
> *Vergilius erat poeta.*
>
> Everyone came down from the Capitoline.
>
> *omnes de Capitolio venerunt.*

In each of these two examples, the verb is also joined by other words that complete its meaning, but in neither instance do we see a direct object: in the first example we have a predicate noun (see §2.1), and in the second a prepositional phrase. In Latin, this means that an intransitive verb will not govern as direct object a noun *in the accusative case*.

It is a feature of English that many verbs can be used both transitively and intransitively with no distinction in form:

> He <u>turned</u> his chair to face the speaker.
>
> He <u>turned</u> when he heard a noise behind him.
>
> I <u>walk</u> the dog every morning.
>
> I <u>walk</u> to school when the weather is nice.

There is no inflectional marker on the verb itself to indicate whether it is being used transitively or intransitively. Latin also has such verbs, but we shall see in the discussion of voice below (§11.5) how the language makes this distinction.

11.1.1 FINE POINTS

We defined transitive verbs as verbs that can take a direct object; intransitive verbs cannot take a direct object. Similarly, sentences can be described as transitive (having a direct object in the main predicate) or intransitive (not having a direct object in the main predicate). This distinction between transitive and intransitive is a useful taxonomic convenience, but it's very inexact and has little real or intrinsic semantic or psychological significance.

Even though a verb *can* take a direct object, it doesn't always do so. When a verb is the only constituent part of sentence's predicate, it's said to be used absolutely. When a verb is used in an expanded predicate that doesn't include a direct object, it's said to be used intransitively. And when a verb is used in a predicate that does include a direct object, it's said to be used transitively. These claims are also true for Latin verbs.

They sang. [absolute use]

They sang out of tune. [intransitive use]

They sang a Welsh folk tune. [transitive use]

Care must be exercised with Latin verbs, however, because often when a verb is used absolutely or intransitively, the English verb used to translate it can be different from the English used to translate the same verb when transitive; for example,

vincunt: They are <u>winning</u>.

facile vincunt: They are <u>winning</u> easily.

Parthos vincunt: They are <u>defeating</u> the Parthians.

Sometimes an English verb that is normally intransitive can be observed to be transitive in a particular restricted usage; for example,

I walked in the road.

I walked the dog in the road.

The verb 'walk' is usually intransitive, except when it means 'to take someone or something for a walk', in which case it is transitive.

Some Latin verbs, commonly used intransitively, can also be found used transitively; if the equivalent verb in English is intransitive, the addition of a preposition into your translation will be required. For example, the verb *gaudeo* 'I rejoice' is normally intransitive, but when it's occasionally used transitively, it must be translated 'I rejoice at'.

An intransitive verb compounded with a prepositional prefix may become transitive. The verb *eo, ire* 'to go', for example, is always intransitive; but when it's compounded with *ad* and becomes *adeo, adire* 'to approach', it can become transitive. The compounded verb, however, may also be used with a preposition, rendering the verb intransitive again. Compare,

urbem adimus: We are approaching the city. [transitive]

ad urbem adimus: We are approaching the city. [intransitive]

A few Latin verbs (compounds or impersonals for the most part) can be observed to be used either in transitive or intransitive sentences, with no discernible difference in meaning. The verb *despero, desperare*, to cite an example, can be found with an object in either the accusative or dative, and in either case it means 'despair for or over':

salutem OR *saluti desperamus.*

We despair for our safety.

Worth special attention are those common intransitive verbs that take nouns in the dative case: *ausculto* 'heed, obey', *auxilior* 'aid, assist', *blandior* 'flatter, gratify', *cedo* 'yield to', *credo* 'believe, trust', *faveo* 'favor', *fido*[2] 'trust, rely on' and *diffido* 'distrust', *gratulor* 'congratulate', *irascor* 'become angry at', *medeor* 'cure, relieve', *minor* 'threaten', *moderor* 'restrain', *noceo* 'harm', *nubo* 'wed', *parco* 'spare', *pareo* 'obey', *permitto* 'allow', *placeo* 'please' and *displiceo* 'displease', *plaudo* 'applaud', *repugno* 'oppose, resist', *resisto* 'resist, reply', *respondeo* 'respond, reply', *servio* 'serve', *studeo* 'be devoted to, pursue', *suadeo* 'urge' and *persuadeo* 'persuade', *tempero* 'refrain from', *vaco* 'be available for/to'.

To be added to this list are many intransitive compound verbs prefixed with *ad* (e.g., *adsentior* 'agree with', *adsum* 'assist, support', *adversor* 'resist, oppose', *appareo* 'appear to', *appropinquo* 'approach'); *ante; con-* (e.g., *confido*[2] 'trust, believe', *consentio* 'be in harmony with, be consistent with'); *de* (e.g., *desum* 'lack'); *in* (e.g., *ignosco* 'forgive', *impero* 'command', *indulgeo* 'indulge, concede', *insidior* 'ambush', *invideo* 'envy, begrudge'); *inter* (e.g., *intersum* 'attend, take part in'); *ob* (e.g., *oboedio* 'heed, obey', *obsequor* 'yield to, gratify, humor', *obsisto*

---

2. *fido* and *confido* are sometimes construed with the ablative instead of the dative.

'block, oppose', *obsto* 'hinder, obstruct', *obsum* 'harm, injure', *obtempero* 'comply with, obey', *obtrecto* 'belittle, decry', *officio* 'oppose, hurt'); *post; prae* (e.g., *praesto* 'surpass', *praestolor* 'wait for', *praesum* 'be in charge of'); *pro* (e.g., *prosum* 'benefit, profit); *sub* (e.g., *subvenio* 'aid, assist', *sufficio* 'suffice', *supplico* 'pray to, worship', *suscenseo* 'be angry at'); and *super* (e.g., *supersum* 'survive; suffice'). Many of these compound verbs can be construed transitively or with a prepositional phrase instead of with the dative.

Also to be noted are those intransitive deponent (see §11.5) verbs, which take nouns in the ablative case: *fruor* 'enjoy', *fungor* 'perform', *potior*[3] 'acquire, get', *utor* 'use', *vescor* 'feed on', and sometimes *epulor* 'feast on'. As vestiges of the middle voice (see §11.5), in early Latin these verbs were sometimes used transitively, a usage that explains why they were occasionally used in perfect passive and future passive participles (see §13) and in passive periphrastics (see §15.3.2).

Finally, a distinctive usage of intransitive verbs in the passive creates an impersonal construction:

in viis pugnatur: There is fighting in the streets.

ventum est: There was a coming.

11.2 VERBAL NOUNS AND ADJECTIVES

Both English and Latin contain a number of verbal nouns and adjectives. These words are paradigmatically derived from verbs but function syntactically as nouns or adjectives. In English, for example, we find the following:

Active participle: <u>Hearing</u> a noise, I went out to investigate.

Passive participle: <u>Summoned</u> by the teacher, the students returned to the classroom.

Gerund:[4] By <u>rowing</u> swiftly the Roman fleet reached Sicily just in time.

Infinitive: Not all citizens wanted <u>to honor</u> Caesar.

---

3. *potior* is sometimes construed with the genitive case instead of the ablative.

4. A **gerund** is a verbal noun that in English always bears the suffix *-ing*.

As these examples show, although they are functioning as nouns or adjectives, their verbal nature allows them to employ some of the syntax of verbs as well: governing direct objects, for example, or adverbial modification.

Latin frequently employs infinitives (§12) and participles (§13); it also has a gerund (§15), which is less common. In addition, Latin has two verbal nouns called supines (§15.1), which are rather rare, as well as an adjective called the gerundive (§15.2), which has several important uses.

11.3 PERSON AND NUMBER

On the model of classical languages, English verbs have traditionally been said to have three persons. However, the concept of **person** isn't often reflected in the main verb itself but rather in the persons or things serving as the subject of the verb:

I walk.

We sing.

We were listening.

I will speak.

In the preceding examples, the persons are 1st person, as exhibited by the use of the 1st person pronouns in the subjective case.

You walk.

You [plural] sing.

You [plural] were listening.

You will speak.

These are all 2nd persons, as exhibited by the use of the 2nd-person pronoun in the subjective case.

These are examples of the 3rd person:

She walks.

They sing.

The people were listening.

The politician will speak.

In these, the use of both nouns and 3rd-person pronouns in the subjective case reveals that the verbs are 3rd person.

Notice that in the 3rd person (singular only) the inflection on the main verb or one of its auxiliaries can change:

I walk. → She walk<u>s</u>.

You were walking. → He <u>was</u> walking.

They are walking. → It <u>is</u> walking.

We have walked. → She <u>has</u> walked

You [plural] do walk. → He <u>does</u> walk.

But

I walked. → She walked.

The feature of number is also present for English verbs. But, again, it is exhibited more by the nouns and pronouns of verbs' subjects than by the inflections on the verbs themselves. In fact, there is no verb inflection in English that specifically signifies number, except for the *-(e)s* suffix generally used in the present singular of the 3rd person (cf. the examples just above).

As is the case with English nouns, verbs in English reflect the numbers of singular and plural but only in the 3rd-person present. In other 3rd person instances, the distinction can be made by means of the auxiliary verbs used:

She read<u>s</u>. → They read.

She <u>was</u> reading. → They <u>were</u> reading.

She <u>has</u> read. → They <u>have</u> read.

To put a fine point on the matter, the only English verb inflection pertaining to person and number is *-(e)s,* which is placed on the 3rd-person singular of simple present verbs; thus, one might say, the English verb actually has only two persons: 3rd singular (in the present only) and all others.[5]

(I) walk.	(We) walk.
(You) walk.	(You all) walk.
(He/She/It) walk<u>s</u>.	(They) walk.

Latin verbs have the same three persons as English verbs (i.e., 1st, 2nd, and 3rd) and distinguish between them by means of inflectional endings.

ambul<u>o</u>: I walk.

can<u>imus</u>: We sing.

audieb<u>as</u>: You were listening.

loqu<u>emini</u>: You [plural] will speak.

ambula<u>vit</u>: He/She/It has walked.

cecin<u>erunt</u>: They did sing.

Several things should be borne in mind with person and number for Latin verbs. First, subjects consisting of collective nouns, which though semantically plural are grammatically singular, are usually construed with singular verbs.

The people <u>are</u> angry: *populus <u>est</u> iratus.*

Next, compound subjects in Latin, as in English, typically take plural verbs. A 1st-person plural verb is used if one of the subjects is 1st person; absent a 1st person, a 2nd-person plural verb is used if one or more of the subjects is 2nd person:

Both Nero and Britannicus were Seneca's students.

  et Nero et Britannicus <u>erant</u> discipuli Senecae.

Both Nero and I were Seneca's students.

  et ego et Nero <u>eramus</u> discipuli Senecae.

---

5. The only exceptions to this are the verb 'to be', which uses 'am' in the 1st-person present (contrast 'is' in the 3rd singular and 'are' everywhere else in the present) and 'was' in the 1st- and 3rd-persons past (contrast 'were' everywhere else in the past); the auxiliary verb 'will', according to formal English grammar, is used in the 2nd and 3rd persons (singular and plural) but is to be replaced by 'shall' in the 1st person (singular and plural).

Both you and I were Seneca's students.
et ego et tu eramus discipuli Senecae.

Both you and Nero were Seneca's students.
et tu et Nero eratis discipuli Senecae.

Third, as in English, two singular subjects that are thought of as forming a unit or a whole can be construed with a singular verb in Latin.

Peanut butter and jelly is my favorite sandwich.

Time and necessity demand this: *tempus necessitasque hoc postulat.*

11.4 ASPECT AND TENSE

Consider the following series of sentences, arranged according to the conventional differentiation into six verb tenses:

Present: I believe what you say. [SIMPLE FACT IN THE PRESENT]
   The neighbor's dog is barking. [PROGRESSIVE ACTION IN THE PRESENT]
   I walk the dog every morning. [REPEATED ACTION]
   Love conquers all. [TIMELESS TRUTH]
   I do love you. [EMPHATIC OR ONGOING]

Past: The ships sailed at dawn. [SIMPLE FACT IN THE PAST]
   The Argonauts were sailing through the Hellespont. [PROGRESSIVE ACTION IN THE PAST]
   We used to visit Baiae every summer. [REPEATED ACTION IN THE PAST]
   I did love you. [PAST EMPHATIC OR ONGOING]

Future: We will leave for Sicily tomorrow morning. [SIMPLE ACTION IN THE FUTURE]
   We will be sailing all day. [PROGRESSIVE ACTION IN THE FUTURE]
   I will walk the dog daily. [REPEATED ACTION IN THE FUTURE]

Present Perfect: Seneca has arrived. (= Seneca is here.)
   I have learned Latin. (= I know Latin.)

Past Perfect: By evening, Seneca <u>had arrived</u>. (= Seneca <u>was</u> there in the evening.)

By age twelve, I <u>had learned</u> Latin. (= I <u>knew</u> Latin at age twelve.)

Future Perfect: By this time tomorrow, Seneca <u>will have arrived</u>. (= Seneca <u>will be</u> here by this time tomorrow.

By the time I am twenty, I <u>will have learned</u> Latin. (= I <u>will</u> <u>know</u> Latin when I am twenty.)

Although the word **tense** is derived from the Latin word *tempus,* meaning 'time', it is clear that the distinction among these verbal phrases involves more than simple chronology. There are, after all, only three logical possibilities for the chronological relationship between an event or state of being and its being reported: prior (past), contemporaneous (present), and subsequent (future). There is another type of differentiation at work in these sentences, one that grammarians often call **aspect**. What is indicated by the aspect of a verb form is not the time, relative to the speaker, that its action takes place but the type of action that it is (ongoing, habitual, one time, complete, or incomplete) and whether the speaker wishes to call attention to the action itself or to its result upon completion. Consequently, in addition to the three possible "tenses" as narrowly defined chronologically, there are three possible aspects:

(1) The **imperfective** aspect is that of an action that is ongoing or habitual and thus not viewed as completed (the name comes from the Latin word for 'unfinished'). In the examples above, the verbs in all of the sentences designated present are imperfective in aspect, since none describes an action or state of being that has been completed. In general, present tense verbs will be imperfective, since they are simultaneous with the reporting of them and hence must still be going on.[6] In the sentences designated above as past, the last three all relate uncompleted actions, since they describe situations as either

---

6. Some special cases might be seen as exceptions to this. In sentences containing a verb in the so-called **historical present**, the action is actually in the past although the verb tense is present (generally employed for enhanced liveliness), so it may well be a completed action at the time of reporting ('So I stop at the library on the way home, and who do you think I see there. . . ?'). Other examples are jokes ('A guy walks into a bar with a penguin. . . .') and narratives of hypothetical situations ('A man's son desperately needs a life-saving drug, but he can't afford to buy it, so he breaks into a pharmacy. . . .'), where the present tense verb describes actions that are timeless, rather than simultaneous with their narration. Similarly, the present tense is often used in literary discussion to describe the actions of fictional characters ('In a fit of madness, Hamlet kills Polonius hiding behind the arras. . . .').

ongoing ('were sailing', 'did love') or repeated ('used to visit'). Thus their aspect is imperfective. Similarly, a sentence envisioning an ongoing, incomplete action in the future will contain a verb with imperfective aspect ('will be sailing').

(2) The **perfective** aspect, as you might expect (this name coming from the Latin word for 'completed'), emphasizes the completion of the action, and the ongoing results—status rather than process. It can apply to actions in the present, past, or future, as noted in the examples above. In essence, the result that the speaker wants to call attention to will be one chronological step closer to the present than the action expressed by the verb. 'Seneca has arrived' is a statement made about the present ('Seneca is here') by expressing a completed action in the past; hence the designation "present" perfect. So too, 'Seneca had arrived' makes a statement about the past ('Seneca was there') with a verb whose action took place at an even earlier point in time.

(3) There remains one other logical possibility: a verb expressing an action as a simple fact or event, with no reference to completeness or repetition. Here the traditional terminology employed in English syntax lets us down, and so we will anticipate the forthcoming discussion of a Latin verb and designate this third and final aspect as the **aoristic** aspect. Since present tense verbs, for reasons given above, are almost always imperfective, the aoristic aspect is largely confined to verbs expressing past and future events. In the case of the former, such verbs are often said to be in the "simple past," as opposed to the imperfective or perfective past. 'The ships sailed at dawn' is an example of a sentence with an aoristic verb.

This system of tenses and aspects is fairly straightforward (not to say, rather elegant and economical): three chronological tenses, each of which can theoretically be combined with three different aspects—nine possibilities. The situation only becomes muddled because the word "tense" is habitually used loosely to refer to both time and aspect. This is true not only in descriptions of English syntax, where the term *aspect* is not even employed, but also in Latin, where it is employed only rarely. So the beginning student will learn that there are six "tenses" for the Latin verb: present, imperfect, future, perfect, past perfect (or pluperfect, as it is often called), and future perfect. This taxonomy very closely approximates the English one delineated above and in fact conceals virtually the same tense versus aspect distinctions. The only difference is that whereas English uses auxiliary verbs to mark these distinctions, Latin employs inflectional affixation (except in the perfect passive system).

Notice how in Latin nearly every "tense" can display a variety of aspects:

PRESENT:	*dormit*	He sleeps. [aoristic]
		He is sleeping. [imperfective]
		He does sleep. [aoristic or imperfective]
FUTURE:	*dormiet*	He will sleep. [aoristic]
		He will be sleeping. [imperfective]
IMPERFECT:	*dormiebat*	He was sleeping. [imperfective]
		He used to sleep. [imperfective]
		He kept sleeping. [imperfective]
		He was trying to sleep. [imperfective]
PERFECT:	*dormivit*	He slept. [aoristic]
		He has slept. [perfective]
		He did sleep. [aoristic or imperfective]
FUTURE PERFECT:	*dormiverit*	He will have slept. [perfective]
PLUPERFECT:	*dormiverat*	He had slept. [perfective]

Latin's ability to accommodate all these rather unruly variations neatly into its six "tenses" bears out the previous claim of elegance and economy. The only challenge this system poses is choosing the best variation for your translations, which isn't especially difficult when a verb is found in context.

The following table shows how these temporal and aspectual possibilities are combined in the six Latin "tenses" (designated in upper case):

	Imperfective	Aoristic	Perfective
Present	PRESENT	PRESENT	PERFECT
Past	IMPERFECT	PERFECT	PLUPERFECT
Future	FUTURE	FUTURE	FUTURE PERFECT

Or, to present the same information with a different orientation:

LATIN TENSES	POTENTIAL ASPECTS
Present	Imperfective or Aoristic
Future	Imperfective or Aoristic
Imperfect	Imperfective
Perfect	Aoristic or Perfective
Pluperfect	Perfective
Future Perfect	Perfective

Some things to note:

(1) From the standpoint of morphology, we often make reference to two different "systems": the **present system** refers to the verb endings found in the present, future, and imperfect tenses, while the **perfect system** refers to the verb endings in the perfect, future perfect, and pluperfect tenses.

(2) The Latin perfect tense actually represents a historical conflation of two distinct Indo-European "tenses": the perfect and the aorist (a "tense" found in ancient Greek). This is the reason a verb like *dixi* can be translated as 'I have said' (true perfect) or as 'I said' or 'I did say' (aoristic perfect). Evidence of the Indo-European perfect can be observed in the reduplication in the perfect active system of many verbs, for example, *curro, currere, cucurri*. Evidence of the Indo-European aorist can be observed in the *-s-* in the perfect active system of many verbs: *scribo, scribere, scripsi*. Apart from being an interesting historical artifact, the Latin conflation of the Indo-European perfect and aorist will have syntactical implications when we examine indirect statements (see §16).

(3) The nonpast tenses—the present, true perfect, future, and future perfect—are called the **primary tenses**; and the imperfect, aoristic perfect, and pluperfect tenses are called the **secondary tenses**. This distinction will become relevant in the syntax of subordinate clauses, where a sentence whose main clause contains a verb in a primary tense will be said to constitute a **primary sequence** and a sentence whose main verb is in a secondary tense will be said to constitute a **secondary sequence**. The entire system whereby certain tenses trigger each particular sequence is referred to as the **complete rules for the sequence of tenses** (see §11.7.3).

(4) Although we talk about "tenses" for the non-indicative moods (imperative and subjunctive) and participles and infinitives, they should not be thought of

as referring strictly to time. They sometimes indicate aspect, not time; and they sometimes designate things sequential—that is, whether an event is prior to, contemporaneous with, or subsequent to the context or the main verb.

(5) It is particularly important to understand clearly the difference between the imperfect and perfect "tenses" when talking about the past. The imperfect is used for the description of circumstances, general information, habitual or ongoing actions, or the endeavor (perhaps ultimately unsuccessful) to perform an action. The perfect is employed for the factual statement of actions that are discrete events, successfully completed. For example, 'Once upon a time there was a kingdom ruled by a wise and kindly king who had a beautiful daughter. She was so beautiful that young men from miles around repeatedly came and sought her hand in marriage. Then one day, a mysterious stranger rode up to the castle and asked to speak with the king. . . .' All of the underlined verbs in the first two sentences would be in the imperfect tense, those in the last sentence in the perfect.

(6) There are instances in which the tenses are used seemingly in violation of their chronological sense. Similar to the English examples given in footnote 6, above, Latin offers a **historical present** to increase the drama or liveliness of a narrative. The present is also on occasion used for future events, especially colloquially in questions and conditions. The perfect is sometimes used in place of the present in statements of general truth, a use designated as the **gnomic perfect**. The future tense can often be found, as in English, as an equivalent of the imperative: 'You will eat your dinner!' In the so-called **epistolary tenses**, the writer of a letter sometimes adopts the chronological standpoint of the reader in the future and uses the imperfect and perfect tenses in place of the present tense and the pluperfect tense instead of the imperfect and perfect tenses to describe circumstances relative to the time of writing.

(7) The auxiliaries 'do' and 'did' in the present and past are usually referred to as an aoristic emphatic (e.g., 'I did do my homework!'), but their use in interrogatives (e.g., 'Did you do your homework?') reveals that their usage isn't always emphatic.

(8) Perfect progressives in English (e.g., 'I have been sleeping', 'I had been sleeping', and 'I will have been sleeping'), which are imperfective in aspect, are met in Latin with no exact counterparts. If a Latin author wished to underscore imperfectiveness in the remote past, he could attempt to do so by means of adverbs and/or prepositional phrases.

11.5 VOICE

The grammatical characteristic of **voice** expresses an important concept for verbs. Since verbs typically involve the notion of action, voice addresses the issues of where the action of the verb originates and where it ends. In some constructions, an action originates from the grammatical subject. In others, the action ends at the grammatical subject. And in still others, the action both originates and ends at the subject. These differences in "verbal trajectory" are crucial for understanding the concept of voice.

There are two different voices commonly found in Latin: active and passive. They are usually distinguished by means of inflectional endings. Indo-European, Latin's parent language, also had a so-called middle voice, traces of which can occasionally be found in Latin.

In an **active** construction, the action simply originates outward from the subject:

> He looked. *spectavit.*

> They will stop the enemy. *hostes prohibebunt.*

In **passive** constructions, the action of the verb acts on the subject. Thus, the subject receives the verb's action, which has originated elsewhere:

> We were looked at. *spectati sumus.*

> They will be stopped by the enemy. *ab hostibus prohibebuntur.*

In a **middle** construction, the action originates from the subject but then in some way "boomerangs" back to the subject. Thus, the subject is acting on or for itself. In Latin prose, this idea is usually expressed by means of a reflexive; in Latin poetry, this can occasionally be expressed with a verb that appears to be passive but takes a reflexive direct object nonetheless.

> He looked at himself. *se spectavit.*

> They will wash their own hands. *manus lavabuntur.* [POETIC]

The active and passive voices are familiar enough to English speakers. You may have even had the experience of being instructed not to use the passive voice in your writing. True, a passive constructive may lack specificity, but an artful writer can, at well-chosen moments, intend to be somewhat vague.

In English, we can express middle-voice concepts with the use of reflexive pronouns:

He looked <u>at himself</u> in the mirror.

They will enjoy <u>themselves</u> skiing.

Notice how if the preceding reflexives had been omitted, the sense of the sentences wouldn't be much affected.

Sometimes, a middle idea can be inherent in certain verbs. For example, when you're told, 'Wash before dinner!', you know to wash *yourself*. If a headline reads, 'America Defends against Terrorism', you know that America is defending *itself*.

Finally, English can use a construction with the auxiliary verb 'get' to express the idea of the middle voice (i.e., a "verbal trajectory" medial between the active and passive voices):

Jill got herself promoted.

Those guys got themselves caught in a sting operation.

Notice the semantic differences between the preceding and their passive and active counterparts:

Jill was promoted.

The boss promoted Jill.

Those guys were caught in a sting operation.

A sting operation caught those guys.

You can see how in the middle construction, the subjects are implied to play a greater role in the actions of being promoted or being caught than the active and passive constructions convey.

Back to Latin again: the inflectional forms of active verbs are unique; the inflectional forms of passive verbs are unique; and the rare occurrence of the middle voice reveals forms identical with the passive.

Latin active (and middle) verbs may, or may not, take a direct object; true passive verbs do not.[7] Certain Latin verbs, called **deponent verbs**, occur *only* in the passive forms in all tenses; they do commonly take a direct object. Most deponent verbs seem to have an active sense and no discernible passive or middle force at all. That is, it isn't really evident by their usage that deponents' meaning implies reflexivity or self-benefit (the hallmark features of the middle voice) or passivity; rather, they seem to be active in everything but form. The existence of deponent verbs is probably a vestige of the Indo-European parent language, while many of the verbs themselves that became deponents probably did so only as a matter of development and popular usage.

For a small class of verbs, passive forms are employed exclusively in particular tenses, while in other tenses forms of the active voice are found. These verbs are sometimes referred to as **semi-deponents**. Usually, their forms are active in the present system, and they use passive forms in the perfect system; these verbs may be more middle (e.g., reflexive) in meaning and a direct object is even allowed with them (which is atypical of true passives).

Deponents and semi-deponents, because they're lacking some forms, will have distinctive principal parts. Exercise special care in learning them. Deponents' dictionary entries always list them under their present passive form.

The passive forms of some verbs can disguise a true middle meaning. For example, the verb *vertere* means 'to turn' in the active, but when it's found in the passive, *verti*, it often means 'to turn oneself' rather than 'to be turned'. Similarly, *pascere* means 'to give nourishment to', but *pasci* often means 'to feed oneself'.

A group of approximately twenty common verbs in Latin are found both in the active and as deponents with no discernible difference in meaning, for example,

merere/mereri: to earn   *metare/metari:* to measure off

comperire/comperiri: to discover   *miserere/misereri:* to pity

---

7. The only exception to this rule is verbs that take double accusative direct objects (e.g., some verbs: 'to teach', 'to ask', 'to conceal from'), where one object is a person and the other a thing. When such a verb is used in the passive voice, the person is changed into the nominative case, while the accusative is retained for the thing:

hanc artem nos docebant: They were teaching us this skill.
hanc artem docebamur: We were being taught this skill.

The presence of an accusative direct object will indicate that the verb is deponent and not passive.

Some Latin verbs have a common meaning in the active voice and a different and distinct meaning in the passive or middle voice. Often, the meaning in the passive/middle is more specialized or restricted.

videre: to see	*ferre:* to bear
videri: to seem	*fertur:* it is reported
facere: to make, to do	*tradere:* to hand over
fieri: to become	*traditur:* it is reported
vehere: to carry	*habere:* to have
vehi: to ride, drive	*haberi:* to be considered

One voice (the active) is transitive, while the other voice (the passive) is typically intransitive.

Finally, it's worth noting that Latin, unlike English, shows no overall avoidance of the passive voice. And when we examine deponent/active doublets (i.e., verbs that are virtually synonymous), no real preference emerges. Notice that almost all of the most common deponents could be replaced with common active verbs; for example,

catch, gain, attain: *adipiscor, adipisci* or *capio, capere*

think, suppose: *arbitror, arbitrari* or *opinor, opinari* or *reor, reri* or *cogito, cogitare* or *existimo, existimare* or *puto, putare*

try, attempt: *conor, conari* or *tempto, temptare*

test, make trial of: *experior, experiri* or *attempto, attemptare* or *probo, probare*

acknowledge, admit: *fateor, fateri* or *agnosco, agnoscere*

enjoy: *fruor, frui* or *gaudeo, gaudere*

do, perform, discharge: *fungor, fungi* or *facio, facere* or *ago, agere*

step, go: *gradior, gradi* or *eo, ire*

urge, encourage: *hortor, hortari* or *insto, instare* or *urgeo, urgere* copy, imitate: *imitor, imitari* or *simulo, simulare*

slip, sink, fall: *labor, labi* or *cado, cadere*

speak, converse: *loquor, loqui* or *for, fari* or *fabulor, fabulari* or *verba facere* or *orationem habere* or *dico, dicere*

fight, struggle: *luctor, luctari* or *pugno, pugnare* or *contendo, contendere*

threaten: *minor, minari* or *impendeo, impendere* or *immineo, imminere*

build, move: *molior, moliri* or *moveo, movere*

die: *morior, mori* or *pereo, perire*

delay, stay, loiter: *moror, morari* or *maneo, manere*

find, obtain, get: *nanciscor, nancisci* or *invenio, invenire*

be born, grow: *nascor, nasci* or *cresco, crescere*

lean on, strive, exert oneself: *nitor, niti* or *incumbo, incumbere* or *laboro, laborare*

begin, undertake: *ordior, ordiri* or *incipio, incipere* or *suscipio, suscipere*

arise, occur: *orior, oriri* or *incido, incidere* or *accido, accidere*

suffer: *patior, pati* or *fero, ferre*

promise: *polliceor, polliceri* or *promitto, promittere*

acquire, get: *potior, potiri* or *capio, capere* or *habeo, habere*

pray, entreat: *precor, precari* or *oro, orare* or *peto, petere* or *quaero, quaerere*

set out: *proficiscor, proficisci* or *procedo, procedere*

follow, pursue: *sequor, sequi* or *insisto, insistere*

see, watch, guard: *tueor, tueri* or *video, videre* or *specto, spectare* or *servo, servare*

punish, avenge: *ulciscor, ulcisci* or *vindico, vindicare* or *punio, punire*

use, employ, handle, possess: *utor, uti* or *adhibeo, adhibere* or *confero, conferre* or *tracto, tractare* or *habeo, habere*

worship, honor: *veneror, venerari* or *colo, colere*

fear: *vereor, vereri* or *metuo, metuere* or *timeo, timere*

eat, feed on: *vescor, vesci* or *edo, esse/edere* or *comedo, comesse/comedere*

Intellectually, the concept of voice in Latin exhibits some fascinating nuances. But practically, voice poses very few problems for students.

11.6 NEGATION

An English declarative sentence is most simply negated with the adverb 'not'. The syntax of negation differs, however, depending on whether or not there is an auxiliary in the sentence.

If an auxiliary verb is present, the negating adverb is placed directly after it:

The ship is departing.

The ship is <u>not</u> departing.

We will go to the theater tonight.

We will <u>not</u> go to the theater tonight.

I have seen that play before.

I have <u>not</u> seen that play before.

If the sentence contains a simple verb, it is the emphatic form of the sentence that is negated, with the auxiliary verb 'do':

I see what you mean. → I <u>do</u> see what you mean. → I <u>do</u> <u>not</u> see what you mean.

The speaker persuaded the jury. → The speaker <u>did</u> persuade the jury. → The speaker <u>did</u> <u>not</u> persuade the jury.

When you are translating such a negated sentence into Latin, it is important to remember that there will be no word in the Latin corresponding to the English 'do' or 'did'.

In addition to the adverb 'not', English can alternatively express negation through the use of other negative adverbs and pronouns, such as 'nobody', 'nowhere', 'never', etc. The key word here is *alternatively:* in a given sentence one or the other negative may be used but not both (which results in the colloquialism known as the double negative):

I <u>do</u> <u>not</u> trust anybody in that family. or I trust <u>nobody</u> in that family.

This plan is <u>not</u> going anywhere. or This plan is going <u>nowhere</u>.

If on occasion a double negative is intentionally used, the negatives cancel each other, resulting in a positive statement.

We <u>can't</u> just do <u>nothing</u>. (i.e., We must do something.)

The negation of imperatives follows the same rule as that of sentences with simple verbs. It is the strengthened form of the imperative, with the auxiliary *do*, that is negated:

Tell the children this story. → <u>Do</u> tell the children this story. → <u>Do</u> <u>not</u> tell the children this story.

Here again, there will be no word in Latin prohibitions corresponding to the English *do*.

Latin possesses two simple negating adverbs, *non* and *ne*. They are usually placed directly before the verb that they negate.

navis appropinquat: The ship approaches.

navis <u>non</u> appropinquat: The ship does <u>not</u> approach.

hanc fabulam omnibus dicat: Let her tell this story to all.

hanc fabulam omnibus <u>ne</u> dicat: Let her <u>not</u> tell this story to all.

Generally, *non* is used to negate factual assertions with verbs in the indicative mood and with participles and infinitives. Subjunctives are generally negated with *ne* but sometimes *non*, depending on the syntactic situation. The appropriate choice of negative in each case will be noted as each of these constructions is discussed below. Imperatives (commands) aren't typically negated; instead, negative commands (prohibitions) have their own construction, as we'll see below.

Like English, Latin also has a full range of other negative adverbs and pronouns. Most of them are derivatives of *ne* (*non* itself is derived from *ne unum*).

<u>nemo</u> regem amat. [*nemo* < *ne homo*]
  <u>No one</u> loves the king.

huic viro malo <u>numquam</u> pareamus.

Let us <u>never</u> obey this evil man.

Other negative particles, conjunctions, and adverbs include *nec, neque, neve,* and *neu* 'nor'; *quin* [< *qui-ne*] 'why not?'; *nusquam* 'nowhere'; *numquam* 'never'; *nedum* 'not to say'; *haud* and *minime* 'not at all'.

As in English, double negatives in Latin sentences are grammatically acceptable only when they cancel out the negativity. If a negative compound (e.g., words meaning 'never', 'nowhere', 'nothing', and the like) precedes a simple negative, the result is a positive statement:

nihil non vidi.

I saw something. [literally: I didn't see nothing]

In a figure called **litotes**, two canceling negatives can be used in poetry and high prose to express an emphasized positive:

numquam non audio.

I listen always. [i.e., 'not never' = 'always']

With certain verbs, particularly verbs of speaking or thinking, the negative *non* negates the meaning of the verb, not the subordinate clause that follows (a different negating verb will express that):

Senecam esse sapientissimum non dixi.

This sentence means 'I did not say that Seneca is the wisest', but it implies rather that the speaker thought it or knew it, etc., without actually saying it. On the other hand, *Senecam esse sapientissum negavi* means 'I denied that Seneca was the wisest' or 'I said that Seneca wasn't the wisest', which is a much stronger statement. Although a sentence like *Senecam non esse sapientissimum dixi* is grammatically acceptable and semantically equivalent to *Senecam esse sapientissum negavi*, it is less idiomatic.

11.7 MOOD

The **mood** of a verb form reflects the way the speaker wants the action or condition expressed by the verb to be understood. In English, there are three verbal moods: indicative, imperative, and subjunctive.

An **indicative** verb form expresses an action or circumstance as a factual assertion:

The Parthians <u>are preparing</u> for battle.

Nero <u>was</u> a student of Seneca.

We <u>will offer</u> a sacrifice to the gods tomorrow.

Note that the assertion does not have to be true but merely expressed in the form of a fact: the sentence "Nero was a student of Confucius" would also require a verb in the indicative mood, even though its assertion is false. Indicative sentences such as these are called **declarative** sentences. The indicative is also used in **interrogative** sentences, where the speaker is asking whether a factual assertion is true or seeking other kinds of information about it:

<u>Are</u> the Parthians <u>preparing</u> for war?

When <u>was</u> Nero a student of Seneca?

Why <u>will</u> we <u>offer</u> a sacrifice to the gods tomorrow?

As its name suggests, the **imperative** mood is employed when the verb is a command or strong request:

<u>Announce</u> this news to the assembly.

Please <u>pass</u> the salt.

These are 2nd-person imperatives. The implied subject of such verbs is the person or persons being addressed by the speaker: if it is one person, the subject is 2nd-person singular; if it is more than one, it is 2nd-person plural. English makes no morphological distinction between the two.

There are situations where the speaker expresses an order to be carried out by a person or persons other than those he is addressing, essentially a 3rd-person imperative. English most commonly uses auxiliary verbs for this:

<u>Have</u> the soldiers <u>arrest</u> anyone who looks suspicious.

I'm busy. <u>Let</u> John <u>do</u> it.

Regarding the second example, it is important not to confuse this use of 'let' with that which means 'permit' or 'allow'. The sense here is not that John is to be *allowed* to do it but that he be *asked* or *required* to do it: an alternative expression would be, "Tell John to do it!"

This word 'let' is also employed in a construction that might be considered a 1st-person imperative, although it is conventionally characterized as **hortatory**:

What shall I do? Let me see.

Let's [= let us] meet tomorrow at noon.

The **subjunctive** mood was once more prevalent in English than it is today, having been largely replaced by the indicative. With it the speaker expresses that the action or state expressed by the verb is not factual but rather hypothetical, potential, wished for, or conditional. The only remaining distinct subjunctive inflectional form in English is the 3rd-person singular of the present tense, where the -(e)s suffix of the indicative is omitted:

Indicative: A good orator speaks clearly.

Subjunctive: It is necessary that a good orator speak clearly.

For the verb 'to be', the subjunctive forms in English are 'be' and 'were':

Be that as it may, I still think you are wrong.

Don't look at me as if I were crazy.

There are a few syntactic constructions in which the subjunctive is still employed in formal contemporary English:

(1) In subordinate clauses after verbs or phrases that express commands, necessity, requests, suggestions, etc.
   The council insisted that he undergo questioning.
   The gods demand that sacrifices be pure.

(2) In the expression of wishes, often in combination with the words 'may' (for possible wishes) or 'if only' (for impossible wishes):
   May she rest in peace.
   If only she were here.

(3) In conditional sentences to express conditions that are either somewhat doubtful or completely contrafactual:
   Were he to do this, what would be his reward? (were he to = if he should)
   If I were you, I would be careful.

(4) In object clauses with verbs of fearing, after the archaic word 'lest':
   I fear lest your dire prediction come true.

The Latin verb also has three moods: indicative, imperative, and subjunctive. With very few exceptions, they are all inflectionally distinct from one another. For imperatives and subjunctives, distinctions of "tense" will often have no temporal significance, indicating instead things like emphasis, likelihood, sequential order, or even aspect.

11.7.1 Indicative: The Latin **indicative** mood has largely the same significance as its English counterpart, marking a statement as a factual assertion or a question of fact:

> *servi in agris laborant.*
> The slaves are working in the fields.

> *Theseus Minotaurum necavit.*
> Theseus killed the Minotaur.

> *quis hoc patri meo dicet?*
> Who will tell my father this?

> *cur veneras?*
> Why had you come?

11.7.2 Imperative: The Latin **imperative** mood differs from the English in several respects: (1) the forms for singular and plural are inflectionally distinct; (2) there are imperative forms in the future as well as in the present; and (3) in the future, there are 3rd-person as well as 2nd-person forms.

> *honora matrem et patrem tuum.*
> Honor your mother and father.

> *diligite vicinum vestrum.*
> Love your neighbor.

> *scribunto discipuli epistulam magistro suo.*
> Have the students write a letter to their teacher.

> *iustitia esto.*
> Let there be justice.

Future imperatives are relatively rare in Latin, found mostly in laws and in archaic literature.

11.7.3 Subjunctive: Verbs in the **subjunctive** mood always refer to future events or states that are potential or indeterminate, rather than those that the speaker feels to be certain (to the extent that the future is ever certain), for which the future indicative is employed. Subjunctive forms are found in the present, imperfect, perfect, and pluperfect tenses.

There are a few situations in which the verb of the main clause will be in the subjunctive mood:

(1) The **hortatory** subjunctive, in the 1st person, and the **jussive** subjunctive, in the 3rd person, are the Latin equivalent of the 'let' construction in English; these are negated with *ne*.

> *pugnemus magna cum virtute.*
>
> Let us fight with great valor.
>
> *equum ne ducat.*
>
> Let her not bring the horse.

(2) Also occurring only in the 1st person, singular or plural, is the **deliberative** subjunctive. It expresses a greater uncertainty than usual on the part of the speaker about what he or she will or should do or else it serves as a purely rhetorical question not necessarily requiring an answer; the construction is negated with *non*.

> *quid iudicibus dicam?*
>
> What am I to say to the jury?
>
> *pugnaremus an fugeremus?*
>
> Were we to fight or flee?

(3) The **potential subjunctive** is regularly used to express past, present, or future potentialities; the construction is negated with *non*.

> *vos illud non putetis.*
>
> You wouldn't think that.
>
> *crederes eum esse magnum hominem.*
>
> You might have believed he was a great person.

(4) The **optative subjunctive**, usually introduced by the word *utinam* or *ut*, expresses an earnest wish. If the wish is attainable, the present subjunctive is used; if unattainable, the imperfect or pluperfect subjunctive. Negate this construction with *ne* or *utinam ne*.

> *utinam canant.*
>
> If only they would sing.

> *utinam ne canerent.*
>
> If only they weren't singing.
>
> *utinam ne cecinissent.*
>
> If only they hadn't sung.

(5) As a variation on the foregoing, in poetry and some colloquial contexts, **prohibitions** (i.e., negative commands), can occasionally be expressed with *ne*.

> *ne credatis hostibus.*
>
> Don't trust the enemy.

Most commonly, the subjunctive mood is used with verbs in subordinate clauses:

Purpose clauses (§20) express the purpose for which the action in the main verb was performed:

> *portas custodiunt ut furem capiant.*
>
> They are guarding the gates in order to catch the thief.

Result clauses (§21) express the outcome when an action is conducted to a certain degree or extent:

> *erant tot milites ut hostes terrerent.*
>
> There were so many soldiers that they frightened the enemies.

Clauses of fearing (§22.2) are used with verbs expressing fear to denote the object of the fear:

> *ne Cyclops nos comedat timeo.*
>
> I fear that the Cyclops will eat us.

Some conditional (§17), concessive (§18), relative (§19), causal (§23), and temporal (§24) clauses, especially ones that are non-factual, are usually put into the subjunctive.

Finally, the subjunctive is employed in certain conditional sentences: in future conditions (to be discussed as **future less vivid**, §17.2) where the speaker feels relatively uncertain that the condition will come to pass, and in unreal conditions (to be discussed as **contrary-to-fact**, §17.3) where it is impossible for the condition to come to pass.

si fortiter pugnemus, respublica nos semper celebret.
If we were to fight bravely, the state would honor us forever.

nonne Dido urbem relinqueret, si regina non esset.
Dido would leave the city, wouldn't she, if she weren't queen.

In complex sentences where main verbs introduce subordinate verbs in the subjunctive, the tenses of the latter are determined by the tenses of the former. This is the so-called sequence of tenses introduced above (see §11.4.(3)). The complete rules for the sequence of tenses are as follows:

MAIN VERB TENSE	SUBJUNCTIVE TENSE
present, future, true perfect, or future perfect	1. present if the action is roughly contemporaneous
	2. perfect if the action is prior to the main verb
imperfect, aoristic perfect, or pluperfect	1. imperfect if the action is roughly contemporaneous
	2. pluperfect if the action is prior to the main verb

If futurity needs to be emphasized with the subordinate verb, a future periphrastic (see §15.3) is employed with the verb 'to be' in the proper tense of the subjunctive.

Finally, it's probably worth adding here that sometimes in a complex sentence when a verb occurs in close context with another verb that is subjunctive, the former verb is "attracted" into the subjunctive mood, even though its own grammar would call for an indicative. This phenomenon is referred to as **subjunctive by attraction**.

12. INFINITIVES

The conjugated verb forms discussed to this point are designated as **finite** forms of the verb. Each form shows (i.e., is bounded by) person, number, voice, tense, and mood and can function as the verb of either an independent or subordinate clause. By contrast, the **infinitive** (from the Latin word for 'unbounded') forms of a verb function most often as verbal nouns and show only tense and voice.

In English, the infinitive is a phrase composed of the word 'to' along with the verb and, in some cases, modal auxiliaries. Transitive English verbs have four infinitives, active and passive, in the present and perfect:

present active:	to see
perfect active:	to have seen
present passive:	to be seen
perfect passive:	to have been seen

As noun phrases, infinitives can function as subject or predicate noun:

To desire happiness is only human.

To be obeyed by the people is more important than to be loved by them.

Never to have seen Rome is never to have lived.

As these examples show, the verbal nature of the infinitive allows it to govern direct objects as well as to be modified by adverbs and prepositional phrases.

English infinitives can also be used as the objects of verbs, in which function they are often labeled **complementary** infinitives:

I want to know the truth.

I hope to see you soon.

I would hate to miss the show.

In these examples, the subject of the infinitive is the same as the subject of the main verb. When this is not the case, and where the subject of the infinitive is expressed by a personal pronoun, it must be in the objective (i.e., accusative) case:

I want <u>them</u> to know the truth.

I would hate for <u>her</u> to miss the show.

Note that the infinitive construction cannot always be maintained when the subject differs from that of the main verb. For the second example above, one would have to substitute a subordinate clause for the infinitive, and its subject would be in the subjective (i.e., nominative) case:

I hope that <u>we</u> see you soon.

Beyond these functions as the subject and object of verbs, infinitives appear in English in a wide variety of contexts. They are often used with adjectives to limit or define the sense in which the adjective applies, as in phrases such as 'happy <u>to see</u> you' or 'eager <u>to return</u>'. They play the same role with certain nouns, for example 'the right <u>to speak</u>', or 'the desire <u>to eat</u>'.

An alternative to the future tense employing the modal 'will' is the use of the infinitive after the participle 'going':

I will set out in the morning.

I am going <u>to set out</u> in the morning.

Infinitives are commonly used to express the purpose for which the action in the main verb is undertaken but only when the subject of the verb and the infinitive are the same:

They sailed to Rhodes (in order) <u>to escape</u> the Parthians.

    but

They sailed to Rhodes so that the Parthians would not capture them.

Certain verbs expressing mental or verbal activity can take an infinitive phrase as an alternative to a subordinate clause introduced by the conjunction *that*. Here again, pronominal subjects of the infinitive must be in the objective case:

I know that <u>he</u> is a fool.

I know <u>him</u> <u>to be</u> a fool.

The assembly declared that <u>they</u> were public enemies.

The assembly declared <u>them</u> <u>to be</u> public enemies.

A Latin verb can have as many as six infinitive forms corresponding to all combinations of the two main voices and the three possible time frames (present, past, future). Note that the different "tenses" of the infinitive can reflect aspectual rather than temporal distinctions:

present active: *scribere* 'to write, to be writing'

present passive: *scribi* 'to be written'

future active: *scripturus esse* 'to be about to write, to be going to write'

future passive: *scriptum iri* 'to be about to be written, to be going to be written'

perfect active: *scripsisse* 'to have written, to have been writing'

perfect passive: *scriptus esse* 'to have been written'

Many of the uses of the infinitive in Latin overlap those in English. The infinitive is a neuter noun that functions as the equivalent of a subject:

> *humanum est errare* [= *error*].
> To err [i.e., error] is human.

The complementary infinitive functions as the object of the main verb:

> *volo tibi dicere.*
> I want to talk to you.

> *in nave manere malumus.*
> We prefer to remain on the ship.

If expressed, the subject of the infinitive is in the accusative case; if the subject of the infinitive is the same as the subject of the main verb, a reflexive pronoun is usually used:

> *volo te mihi dicere.*
> I want you to talk to me.

> *cupit se esse divitem.*
> He wants to be rich.

Precisely because the infinitive lacks a personal subject, it commonly occurs in impersonal constructions:

necesse est comperiri veritatem.
It is necessary to learn the truth.

decet colere iustos.
It is proper to honor the just.

diligere hostes est difficile.
It is difficult to love one's enemies.

With one notable exception (i.e., **prohibitions**; see below), infinitives are negated with *non:*

nos in nave non manere iussit.
He commanded us not to remain on the ship.

non diligere hunc est difficile.
It is difficult not to love this man.

Certain adjectives, especially in poetry, have their meaning refined or limited by the addition of infinitive phrases, as they do in English:

hic iuvenis dignus est ducere filiam meam.
This young man is worthy to marry my daughter.

The infinitive occasionally occurs in poetry to express purpose clauses (see §20):

puer intro it videre quid fiat.
The boy goes inside [in order] to see what's happening.

Like the historical present (see above, §11.4.(6)), the **historical infinitive** in Latin can be employed to heighten a narrative's liveliness or suspense:[1]

in viis urbis heri currere, clamare, acriter pugnare.
In the streets of the city yesterday there was running, there was shouting, and there was fierce fighting.

---

1. It should be noted that when historical infinitives have a subject, it is expressed in the nominative. Thus, this is the only exception to the rule that infinitives' subjects are in the accusative.

Latin, like English, has an **exclamatory infinitive**:

> *videre parentes meos iterum!*
> O, to see my parents once again!

The infinitive is commonly used with the imperatives *noli* (singular) or *nolite* (plural) when a command is negated, thus creating a **prohibition**:

> *milites, nolite vereri!*
> Soldiers, don't be afraid.

> *Anna, noli discedere!*
> Anna, don't leave!

The infinitive is also commonly used in indirect statements, as discussed in §16.2.

13. PARTICIPLES

The most common verbal adjectives are called **participles**. English participles exhibit neither variety nor much frequency. Latin participles, on the other hand, are many and richly varied in their settings and senses. Indeed, it's often said that no good Latin sentence lacks a participle. While that may be an overstatement, it is, in fact, popular sport among Latin students to count participles—it's not hard to find prose sentences with three or four participles!

English has two natural participles: a present active and a perfect passive, for example,

the praising poet

the praised general

The present active participle always has the -*ing* suffix,[1] while the perfect passive usually exhibits the -*(e)d* suffix, though the -*(e)n* suffix (e.g., spoken, taken, known, proven) is also quite common. Other types of perfect passive participles, especially of Germanic origin, can also be found (e.g., met, taught, brought, sung, gone, swum). These irregulars are usually found as the third principal part of verb entries in unabridged English dictionaries.

Other English participles are created with the addition of auxiliaries to imitate the richer array of classical participles, but they often seem formal or even awkward, for example,

the poet having praised [perfect active]

the general being praised [present passive]

the athlete about to be praised [future passive]

Latin participles can be found in three "tenses" (present, future, and perfect) and in both voices (active and passive) but not in every combination. Moreover, aspect is operative in participles, not just the temporal characteristics of tense. Latin participles are more frequent than English participles, then, primarily

---

1. Exercise care in distinguishing this -*ing* suffix, which is used both in gerunds and in present participles in English:

smoking is unhealthy [GERUND: noun]
the smoking gun [PARTICIPLE: adjective]

because there are four of them for the normal verb compared with just two in English. So, the nominative masculine singular participles for the Latin verb *lego, legere,* for example, are as follows:

	ACTIVE	PASSIVE
PRESENT	*legens, -ntis*	————
FUTURE	*lecturus, -a, -um*	*legendus, -a, -um*[2]
PERFECT	————	*lectus, -a, -um*

Translated, these mean

	ACTIVE	PASSIVE
PRESENT	reading	————
FUTURE	about to read	(about) to be read
PERFECT	————	having been read, read

This scheme differs a bit for deponent verbs:

	ACTIVE	PASSIVE
PRESENT	*sequens, -ntis*	————
FUTURE	*secuturus, -a, -um*	*sequendus, -a, -um*
PERFECT	————	*secutus, -a, -um*

Notice the shift in translation for the perfect passive:

	ACTIVE	PASSIVE
PRESENT	following	————
FUTURE	about to follow	(about) to be followed
PERFECT	having followed	————[3]

---

2. Before late Latin, the future passive participle is only rarely used in its pure participial sense; the form is also known as the gerundive, for which see §15.

3. With most deponent verbs, the perfect participle is commonly translated actively; with some other deponents, the perfect participle is commonly translated passively; and with a few deponents, it can be translated either actively or passively. This phenomenon isn't really predictable; it's just a matter of common usage.

Thus, deponent verbs (which by definition are passive in form but active in meaning) exhibit two active participles, one passive participle passive in meaning and one passive participle active in meaning.

As adjectives, Latin participles display the characteristics of case, number, and gender so that they properly agree with the nouns or pronouns they modify:

carmen poetae laudantis: the poem of the praising poet

liber poetae laudato: a book to/for the praised poet

Sometimes the adjectival qualities and sometimes the verbal qualities are emphasized for participles, being verbal adjectives. For example, the phrase 'the running man' tells you *what kind of* man is referred to: a *running* man. Thus, the adjectival force of the participle is here foremost. When English wants to feature the verbal qualities of a participle, the syntax is altered somewhat: the man *running* into the shrine (not the-running-into-the-shrine man). This phrase doesn't really describe the man so much as what he's doing (i.e., running into the shrine).

Latin also sometimes distinguishes between the adjectival and the verbal force of its participles. When functioning as an attributive adjective, the Latin participle can be placed before the substantive; when it's a predicate adjective it typically comes after the verb:

divisa Gallia vinci potest: A divided Gaul can be conquered.

Corinna est admodum amans: Corinna is quite loving.

When the participle functions verbally (which is its most common usage in Latin), it can be found virtually anywhere in its sentence or clause:

Gaul, conquered by barbarians . . .

victa a barbaris Gallia . . .

Gallia a barbaris victa . . .

a barbaris victa Gallia . . .

Gallia victa a barbaris . . .

If the participial phrases above were to be expanded with, for example, the prepositional phrase 'out of Germany' or the adverb 'unexpectedly', Latin word order would exhibit even more numerous variations.

These characteristics—the variable position of the participle and its grammatical expansibility—are probably the greatest reason Latin can seem so foreign to English speakers. Again, smart students of Latin need to break themselves of the English habit of reading exclusively from left to right; the usage of Latin participles often requires students to (temporarily) read sentences or clauses from right to left and even inside out!

Another reason Latin participles are so common is they have a broader semantic range than English participles. 'The running man' has a fairly restricted sense; but *vir currens*, besides meaning 'the running man' can also mean 'the man while/when [he's] running', 'the man since/because [he's] running', 'the man though/although [he's] running', 'the man if [he's] running', or 'the man who's running'. Thus, any Latin participle can potentially have a **temporal, causal, concessive, conditional,** or **relative** force. This requires readers of Latin to be very sensitive to context so that they choose the *best* translation for each participle.

There's one final reason for the frequency of Latin participles: their usage in a broad variety of grammatical and syntactical environments:

(1) Used without nouns (or pronouns), participles often serve as substantives:

currens: the [one] running, the runner

laudatos: the ones praised, the praised [ones]

(2) Future participles can convey the idea of purpose or intention:

periturus ex acie progredior:

I step forth from the battle line [in order] to perish.

(3) Sometimes when a condition (see §17) is implied but the apodosis has been suppressed, a participle is used in its place:

vidimus imperatorem laudatum si modo poetae eum novissent:

We saw the general who would have been praised if only the poets had known him.

sic coacti si Roma ardet, discedere nolunt:

They don't wish to leave, though [they would be] so compelled if Rome is burning.

(4) Probably their most important use, participles are very often found in ablative absolutes (see §14).

As the ultimate testimony of the importance of the participle to Latin, we should note that oftentimes the most significant semantic "load" of Latin is carried not by the finite verbs of a sentence but by the participles.

He appeared, running into the shrine with many pursuers.

accurrens in sacrarium cum multis sequentibus conspiciebatur.

14. ABLATIVE ABSOLUTE

Consider the following sentences:

To tell you the truth, I don't know what the answer is.

That having been said, we need to do something.

With the enemy approaching so near, we must guard the gates.

In each case, the underlined phrase is syntactically isolated from the main clause of the sentence and consequently is called an **absolute** phrase. In English, such phrases can be participial or infinitival.

Latin shows much less variety in its use of absolutes: there's no infinitival absolute, and the participial absolute occurs only in the ablative case.

As the name **ablative absolute** suggests, in this construction a participle and its subject noun or pronoun will be in the ablative case, and that noun is usually grammatically independent of anything in the main clause:

hostibus appropinquantibus, oportet nos portas custodire.
The enemy approaching, we should guard the gates.

In this sentence the absolute phrase is causal (= Since the enemy is approaching . . .). The relationship of the ablative absolute to the main clause can also be temporal, concessive, or conditional and is often most idiomatically translated into English with the appropriate subordinate clause rather than an absolute phrase, which actually comes off as rather vague.

Temporal:

hostibus fugientibus, subito pluit.
While the enemy was fleeing, it suddenly rained.
[better than: With the enemy fleeing, it suddenly rained.]

Concessive:

hostibus fugientibus, tamen oportet nos portas custodire.
Although the enemy is fleeing, we still should guard the gates.
[better than: With the enemy fleeing, we still should guard the gates.]

Conditional:

> *deis volentibus, hostes vincemus.*
>
> If the gods are willing, we will defeat the enemy.
>
> [better than: With the gods willing, we will defeat the enemy.]

The greatest problem posed by Latin ablative absolutes is the fact that classical Latin, unlike most other Indo-European languages (e.g., English, ancient Greek, Sanskrit), lacks present and perfect participles for the verb 'to be'. This means, then, that an ablative absolute can consist of just a noun (or pronoun) and either an adjective or another noun:

> *Caesare aegro, non vincemus.*
>
> Caesar [being] sick, we won't win. → If Caesar is sick, we won't win.

> *Caesare deo, Octavianum nunc venerabamur.*
>
> Caesar [being] a god, we now worshipped Octavian. → Since Caesar was a god, we now worshipped Octavian.

Thus, if an editor isn't generous in the use of commas, these "abbreviated" absolutes may be quite difficult to identify.

15. OTHER VERBAL CONSTRUCTIONS

In this chapter, we'll review three final constructions using verbal nouns and adjectives: the **supine**, the **gerund**, and **future periphrastics**. Let's examine them in an order of increasing frequency.

15.1 SUPINES

If your dictionary or primer cites the fourth principal part of regular verbs as ending in -*um*, that principal part is the so-called **supine**, a verbal noun. It is a fourth declension noun and defective in the sense that it only occurs in the accusative and ablative singular—only two forms! So, for the verb *mitto, mittere, misi, missum*, the two supines are

> *missum* (accusative)
>
> *missu* (ablative)

For each form, there is only one single solitary use. This explains why supines are fairly rare in Latin. There is no exact counterpart in English.

(1) With verbs of motion, the accusative supine is used without a preposition to express the purpose or intended goal of that motion:

> They came (in order) <u>to work</u>.   *laboratum venerunt.*
>
> He approaches (in order) <u>to greet</u> us.   *salutatum nos accedit.*

(2) The ablative supine is employed with certain adjectives as an ablative of respect. The most common of these adjectives are *difficilis, dignus, facilis, gravis, honestus, incredibilis, indignus, iucundus, mirabilis, optimus, turpis*, and *utilis*.

> This weapon is hard to carry.   *hoc telum est difficile latu.*
>
> The story is disgraceful to tell.   *fabula est turpis dictu.*

15.2 GERUNDS

As a neuter singular noun of the 2nd declension, the **gerund** is essentially identical to the oblique cases of the neuter singular future passive participle. It usually corresponds to the English gerund ending in -ing. The gerund forms of *gaudere* are the following:

GENITIVE: *gaudendi*

musica est pars gaudendi: Music is part of rejoicing.

DATIVE: *gaudendo*

gaudendo praeest: She is in charge of the rejoicing.

ACCUSATIVE: *gaudendum*

dei nos ad gaudendum vocant: The gods call us to rejoice.

ABLATIVE: *gaudendo*

dei gaudendo fruuntur: The gods enjoy rejoicing.

The verbal quality of a gerund can be exhibited by the addition of an object, a prepositional phrase, or an adverbial modifier:

musica est pars bene gaudendi: Music is part of rejoicing <u>well</u>.

gaudendo post proelium praeest: She is in charge of the rejoicing <u>after the battle</u>.

dei gaudendo laudem fruuntur: The gods enjoy rejoicing at <u>praise</u>.

Examine the previous sentence carefully. Not only does the gerund resemble the gerundive (future passive participle), but they are both used almost interchangeably in several constructions. The following Latin sentence is semantically identical to the previous one:

dei gaudenda laude fruuntur: The gods enjoy rejoicing at praise.
[Literally, the gods enjoy sacrifices to be rejoiced at.]

While a gerund that takes a direct object is perfectly grammatical as a construction, Latin idiom actually prefers the substitution of the object and a gerundive in whatever case the ambient grammar dictates. Notice how *gaudenda laude,* the object and gerundive above, is ablative because of the verb *fruor.*

Gerunds and gerundives can also be used to express purpose. The most common way is with the preposition *ad:*

> *ad epulandum venerunt:* They came (in order) to feast.

> *ad epulandum boletos venerunt:* They came (in order) to feast on mushrooms.

Or preferably,

> *ad epulandos boletos venerunt*

Alternatively, the postpositive prepositions *gratia* and *causa* with the genitive express the same idea.

> *epulandi causa/gratia venerunt:* They came (in order) to feast.

> *epulandi boletos causa/gratia venerunt:* They came (in order) to feast on mushrooms.

Or preferably,

> *epulandorum boletorum causa/gratia venerunt*

15.3 FUTURE PERIPHRASTICS

Future periphrastics represent one of the most adaptable and interesting locutions in Latin. They come in two different varieties: active periphrastics and passive periphrastics.

15.3.1 Active Periphrastics: Future active periphrastics consist of forms of the future active participle together with forms of the verb 'to be' to express a verbal idea intermediate between the present and future in time. The best translation for these periphrastics includes auxiliaries like 'about to', 'going to', or 'on the point of'.

> *discessuri sumus:* We are about to leave.

> *dormiturae erant:* They were on the point of sleeping.

> *pugnaturus est:* He is going to fight.

In subjunctive constructions (see §§18–24), future active periphrastics are frequently employed to convey an idea of futurity.

timeo ne venturi sint: I am afraid that they will come.

15.3.2 Passive Periphrastics: The best translation for future passive periphrastics includes auxiliaries like 'must', 'should', 'ought' or anything expressing duty, necessity, or obligation. This construction requires the gerundive (future passive participle) and forms of the verb 'to be'.

When the verb is transitive, the gerundive agrees with the subject.

cibus mittendus est: Food should be sent.

regina est capienda: The queen must be captured.

fur puniendus erat: The thief had to be punished.

villae erunt vendendae: The houses will have to be sold.

When the verb is intransitive, the gerundive is put in the neuter nominative singular and the construction becomes impersonal.

vivendum est: It is necessary to live.

dormiendum erit: It will be necessary to sleep.

erat pugnandum: It was necessary to fight.

When agency is expressed within a passive periphrastic, a simple dative is used.

cibus domino mittendus est: Food should be sent by the master.

regina tibi est capienda: The queen must be captured by you.

vivendum nobis est: It is necessary for us to live.

liberis dormiendum erit: It will be necessary for the children to sleep.

Be careful with a potential ambiguity that arises when one of the intransitive verbs used with the dative case (see §11.1.1) occurs in a passive periphrastic:

illis parendum est.
    It is necessary for them to obey *or* It is necessary to obey them.

Context will invariably clear up the ambiguity, offering the best of the two possible translations.

16. INDIRECT DISCOURSE

16.1 INDIRECT STATEMENTS

There are two ways to report the content of what a person says or thinks, referred to as **direct** and **indirect statement**. Suppose Caesar says or thinks the following sentence:

Rome is the capital of the world.

If a narrator wants to report what Caesar said or thought, he can do it through **direct statement**, reproducing the words of the original without change:

Caesar said, "Rome is the capital of the world."

Caesar thought to himself, "Rome is the capital of the world."

Or he can use the construction here defined as **indirect statement**, which entails embedding the original statement in a subordinate clause introduced by 'that' (though the conjunction is often omitted in informal speech and writing):

Caesar said that Rome is/was the capital of the world.

Caesar thought that Rome is/was the capital of the world.

The choice between present and past tenses of the verb in the indirect statement depends on whether or not the statement is felt to have ongoing validity at the time it is being reported.

The use of indirect statement often requires changes in the exact wording of the original. A change of subject in the reported speech might be necessary:

"I am a great lover of Rome."

Caesar said that he was a great lover of Rome.

As this example also shows, a change in the tense of the verb might be required if a statement about the present or future is reported in the past and it is no longer considered valid at the time of reporting (if Caesar was dead, for example). Some further examples are these:

"I will lead the Romans to victory."

Caesar claimed that he would lead the Romans to victory.

"We Romans have assembled a great fleet."

Caesar boasted that the Romans had assembled a great fleet.

Indirect statement is deployed with a great variety of verbs within the semantic sphere of speaking, thinking, feeling, or perceiving. Some of these verbs admit the substitution of an infinitive phrase in place of the subordinate clause:

I feel that this is true.

I feel this to be true.

We understand that the time has come.

We understand the time to have come.

If the subject of the infinitive is a pronoun, it will be in the objective case:

"She is a great poet."

We consider her to be a great poet.

For most verbs in this category, however, the infinitive construction is less idiomatic than the subordinate clause.

Latin also permits both the direct and indirect reporting of statements that are spoken, thought, perceived, etc.[1] To return to the example discussed above, if Caesar said,

Roma est caput orbis terrarum.
Rome is the capital of the world,

this can be reported directly:

'Roma', dixit Caesar, 'est caput orbis terrarum'.
Caesar said, "Rome is the capital of the world."

---

1. For future reference, older Latin books sometimes refer to direct statements by the Latin *oratio recta* and indirect statements by *oratio obliqua*.

For the indirect reporting of statements, classical Latin offers only one possible syntactic construction for the reported statement: an infinitive clause.[2] Here too it will be verbs of saying, thinking, perceiving, or feeling that require this construction.

In this construction, if the subject of the infinitive is the same as that of the main verb, it is expressed with a reflexive pronoun in the accusative; if it is different, it too is put in the accusative case. A negative (*non* or *ne*) in the original statement generally remains unchanged. Finally, the finite verb of the direct statement is changed into one of the six available infinitives (though the future passive infinitive is only rarely used), the "tense" of which depends on when that action occurs relative to the timing of the main verb of saying, thinking, perceiving, or feeling. The system is actually quite easy.

(1) Either of the two present infinitives is used when the action expressed by the infinitive is roughly <u>contemporaneous</u> with the action of the main verb:

> I think [today] that Scipio is coming [today].
>
> *puto Scipionem <u>venire</u>.*

(2) Either of the two perfect infinitives is used, when the action expressed by the infinitive is <u>prior</u> to the action of the main verb:

> I think [today] that Scipio came [yesterday].
>
> I think [now] that Scipio has come [previously].
>
> *puto Scipionem venisse.*

(3) And either of the two future infinitives is used when the action expressed by the infinitive is <u>subsequent</u> to the action of the main verb:

> I think [today] that Scipio will come [tomorrow].
>
> *puto Scipionem venturum esse.*

The Latin grammar described in the previous three paragraphs all involved a main verb in one of the primary tenses. The grammar also persists when the main verb is in a secondary tense; the English translation, however, requires some changes.

---

2. In late Latin and spoken Latin, a *quod*-clause can sometimes be observed instead of an infinitive for an indirect statement.

putabam Scipionem venire.   [CONTEMPORANEOUS]
I was thinking [yesterday] that Scipio was coming [yesterday].

putabam Scipionem venisse.   [PRIOR]
I was thinking [yesterday] that Scipio had come [the day before].

putabam Scipionem venturum esse.   [SUBSEQUENT]
I was thinking [yesterday] that Scipio would come [today].

When the perfect passive infinitive or the future active infinitive is used, note two things. First, the form must agree with the subjective accusative:

putabam Scipionem venturum esse.
I was thinking that Scipio would come.

putabam milites venturos esse.
I was thinking that the soldiers would come.

putabam matrem venturam esse.
I was thinking that mother would come.

putabam auxilia ventura esse.
I was thinking that the auxiliaries would come.

Second, the infinitive of the verb 'to be' is commonly omitted, without any change in meaning:

putabam Scipionem venturum.
I was thinking that Scipio would come.

putabam milites venturos.
I was thinking that the soldiers would come.

putabam matrem venturam.
I was thinking that mother would come.

putabam auxilia ventura.
I was thinking that the auxiliaries would come.

16.1.1 Dependent Clauses within Indirect Statement: In many languages, the syntax of dependent clauses within indirect statement is quite complicated, but the rules in Latin are relatively few and straightforward. The rules in modern English, though not numerous, are mostly ignored in everyday speech.

The first thing to understand is the structure of these complex sentences. They consist of at least three major parts: the main clause, the principal clause within the subordinate clause, and the dependent clause within the subordinate clause.

<u>We know</u> that they will show up tomorrow, unless it rains early.
MAIN CLAUSE   SUBORDINATE CLAUSE

        that they will show up tomorrow,   unless it rains early.
        PRINCIPAL CLAUSE   DEPENDENT CLAUSE

In both Latin and English, the syntax of the principal clause is determined by the construction of the indirect statement. That is, for Latin, since the verb of the main clause requires an infinitive, the verb of the principal clause will be an infinitive. Half done, well begun!

On the whole, the verb of the dependent clause is simply put in the subjunctive mood. The tense of the subjunctive is determined by the tense of the verb of the main clause and follows the rule for the sequence of tenses (see §11.7.3):

DIRECT STATEMENT		
Main Clause	Principal Clause of Direct Statement	Subordinate Clause
He thinks,	"The woman is dying	since she is ill."
putat,	*'femina moritur*	*quod est aegra'.*
INDIRECT STATEMENT		
Main Clause	Principal Clause of Indirect Statement	Dependent Clause
He thinks	that the woman is dying	since she is ill.
putat	*feminam mori*	*quod sit aegra.*
He thinks	that the woman is dying	since she has been ill.
putat	*feminam mori*	*quod fuerit aegra.*
He thought	that the woman was dying	since she was ill.
putavit	*feminam mori*	*quod esset aegra.*
He thought	that the woman was dying	since she had been ill.
putavit	*feminam mori*	*quod fuisset aegra.*

16.2 INDIRECT QUESTIONS

An indirect question is a subordinate clause following a verb of knowing, learning, asking, etc. The indirect question is introduced by an interrogative word or phrase and is expressed in Latin by the subjunctive.

DIRECT QUESTION	INDIRECT QUESTION
ubi erant?	*audivit ubi essent.*
Where were they?	He heard where they were.
quis es?	*scimus quis sis.*
Who are you?	We know who you are.

Indirect questions follow the complete rules for the sequence of tenses (see §11.7.3).

16.2.1 Clauses of Doubting: Clauses of doubting are a kind of indirect question. When the doubt is affirmed, the subordinate clause is introduced by the words *num* or *an:*

> *dubito an discedat:* I doubt whether/that he is departing.

> *dubitavi num discederet:* I doubted whether/that he was departing.

A future periphrastic may occur to emphasize futurity:

> *dubito num discessurus sit:* I doubt whether/that he will depart.

> *dubitabam num discessurus esset:* I doubted whether he would depart.

When the doubt is negated, the subjunctive clause is introduced by **quin** 'but that':

> *non dubito quin discedat:* I don't doubt (but) that he is departing.

> *non dubium erat quin discessisset:* There was no doubt that he had departed.

Included in expressions of negated doubt are rhetorical questions like this:

> *quis dubitat quin discedat?:* Who doubts that he is departing?

Since the implication is that <u>no one doubts</u> that he is departing, this is called a virtual or implied negative doubt.[3]

16.3 INDIRECT COMMANDS

In the sentence 'We beg you to conquer', 'to conquer' is an object expressing the indirect command that corresponds to the direct command: 'We beg you: conquer!'

Indirect commands are closely related to purpose clauses: 'We beg (in order) that you conquer'.

The verb of the indirect command is subjunctive, and either of the conjunctions **ut** or **ne** introduce it.

Most verbs of ordering, warning, begging, advising, urging, persuading, requesting, and so forth require this construction.[4]

oramus ut vos vincatis: We beg you to conquer.

imperabat nobis ne discederemus: He was ordering us not to leave.

---

3. When the verb *dubito* is followed by an infinitive, it does not mean 'doubt' but 'hesitate':

dubito discedere: I hesitate to depart.

4. The verbs *iubere* 'to command' and *vetare* 'to forbid' are construed with the infinitive and subjective accusative.

te vincere vetamus: We forbid you to conquer.
me discedere iubebat: He was ordering me to leave.

17. CONDITIONALS

Many linguists and logicians claim that **conditional sentences** are the most difficult "business" any language has to do. This is because conditional sentences reflect contingent thinking and their expression requires a clear distinction between real, potential, and unreal contingencies. Not all practitioners of language fully apprehend the linguistic and/or logical distinctions of these contingencies. Hence the fundamental difficulty.

No language student needs to experience this difficulty if she or he grasps the inherent clarity and structure of conditional sentences. In other words, that area of "language logic" often cited as the most difficult is, in fact, easily comprehensible with the proper analytical tools.

Conditional sentences can be distinguished in terms of their relationship to time, in terms of their relationship to reality, and in terms of their structures and components.

To be more specific, conditional sentences express contingencies that existed (or didn't exist) in the past, that exist (or don't exist) in the present, or that will exist (or may exist) in the future. Likewise, some contingencies are very likely to be fulfilled, others cannot be fulfilled, while still others may or may not be fulfilled.

As to structure, conditionals are typically complex sentences, consisting of a main clause (often called the **apodosis**) and a subordinate clause (often called the **protasis**).

If Caesar attacks, our hopes are over.
[PROTASIS]   [APODOSIS]

The protasis is sometimes referred to as the "if-clause," the "assumption," or the "proposition," while the apodosis can be referred to as the "then-clause," the "conclusion," or the "consequence."[1]

It's worth noting at this juncture that the if-clause (protasis) in English and in Latin doesn't always precede the then-clause (apodosis). In fact, from a

---

1. Etymologically, the Latinate proposition and Greek protasis mean about the same thing: 'a thing set forth'. The Greek apodosis means 'a payoff'.

rhetorical standpoint, sometimes an apodosis that is placed prior to its protasis imparts a greater "punchiness." Consider these examples:

You *will* succeed in life, if you study Latin.

If you study Latin, you will succeed in life.

Basically, the way we distinguish the protasis from the apodosis in English is by means of the conditional subordinating conjunction used in the protasis: 'if', 'unless', etc. Likewise, Latin will always use a subordinating conjunction in the protasis, but like English it will only occasionally use a coordinating conjunction 'then' in the apodosis. Because conditional sentences rely on clauses, clauses rely on verbs, and verbs rely on the notion of tense, students of Latin will find that the principles of tense and aspect (see §11.4) are completely at play in Latin conditionals. That is, theoretically, all of the Latin tenses can be found in factual conditionals. Thus, factual Latin conditionals can be broadly conceived of as operating in the past, present, and future and as occurring as either one-time actions or repeated actions. (Non-factual conditionals will use tense in a slightly different fashion.)

Conditionals can also be classified as real, potential, or unreal. This distinction speaks to their **vividness**, that is, the likelihood of their fulfillment. Unreal conditions cannot be fulfilled, a potential condition may or may not be fulfilled, and a real or factual condition will or won't be fulfilled. In Latin, the distinctions of vividness are made, at least in part, by means of the moods (see §11.7) of the verbs employed in the conditional sentences; in English, the distinctions are made by means of moods and the auxiliary verbs employed.

UNREAL: If it were raining today [but it isn't], they wouldn't play the game.

POTENTIAL: Maybe, if it were to/should rain today, we wouldn't need to water the lawn.

REAL or FACTUAL: Even if it [actually] rains today, the no-burn order is still in effect.

In Latin, the if-word with either the indicative or the subjunctive is *si;* if the protasis is negated, the words meaning 'if not' or 'unless' are *nisi* and *si non*. When the apodosis is negated, *non* is typically used.

17.1 SIMPLE AND GENERAL

The most vivid conditions are called **simple** or **particular conditionals** because they express a fairly direct and automatic vividness between the protasis and apodosis:

If you stick your finger in this light socket, you get a shock.

The directness, or "is-ness," of this relationship naturally relies on the indicative mood, which is, as we saw in §11.7.1, the mood of factual assertion.

General conditionals, inasmuch as they offer a general truth, stay within the indicative realm of "is-ness":

If ever you stick your finger in a light socket, you always get a shock.

17.2 FUTURE

Future conditionals express conditions that will (or will not) be fulfilled in the future. Differences of vividness in English are expressed by the presence (or absence) of auxiliaries used:

More vivid: If you <u>stick</u> your finger in the light socket, you <u>will</u> get a shock.

The protasis here expresses an obvious contingency (i.e., you may or may not stick your finger in the socket), but the contingency is highly "vivid"; so the indicative mood in the future makes sense. The apodosis expresses a future reality, so the future indicative makes sense again.

Less vivid: If you <u>were to/should</u> stick your finger in the light socket, you <u>would</u> get a shock.

Here, the protasis sounds less likely to be fulfilled (i.e., more contingent), thus justifying a subjunctive verb (usually in the present) in Latin. And since the protasis is less likely, the apodosis is similarly remote, and it too justifies a subjunctive (again, in the present).

17.3 CONTRARY-TO-FACT

Finally, some conditions are clearly **contrary-to-fact** (or **contrafactual**) and **unreal**; that is, they have absolutely no likelihood of being fulfilled. Since irreality falls more within the range of maybe-ness than is-ness, and since the subjunctive is the mood of the unreal, it's reasonable to find the subjunctive (imperfect for present contrafactuals, pluperfect for past contrafactuals) used with contrafactual conditions:

> If you had stuck your knee in this light socket [but you didn't], you would have gotten a shock.

17.4 MIXED

Mixed conditionals are sentences that use one type of condition in the protasis and another type in the apodosis. Not uncommon, they are easy enough to identify because each clause conforms to the syntax of its distinct type; for example,

> If Caesar had come, he would be defeating them.
> *si Caesar venisset, eos vinceret.*

Here the protasis is a past contrafactual (notice the pluperfect subjunctive in the Latin), while the apodosis is a present contrafactual (notice the imperfect subjunctive in the Latin). Or, again,

> If Caesar ever comes, he will defeat them.
> *si Caesar venit, eos vincet.*

In this conditional, we find a present general condition in the protasis (notice the present indicative in the Latin) and a future more vivid in the apodosis (notice the future indicative).

Similarly, conditions can be found in sentences of mixed syntax. For example,

> If Caesar is coming, defeat him!
> *si Caesar venit, eum vincite!*

Here we have a present simple condition in the protasis, but the apodosis consists of an imperative. Or, again,

If Caesar should come, what are we to do?

si Caesar veniat, quid agamus?

The protasis in this case reflects a future less vivid condition, but the apodosis presents a deliberative subjunctive (see §11.7.3).

Sometimes, the protasis of a conditional sentence can be expressed by means of a participle, especially in a ablative absolute:

If Caesar is coming, we will retreat.

Caesare veniente, nos recipiemus.

See §§13 and 14 for more discussion on this construction.

Finally, note again that Latin uses different negations for the protasis (*nisi* or *si non*) and the apodosis (*non*).

As you review the following conditional sentences, which exemplify all the different types, pay careful attention to the moods, tenses, aspects, particles, and conjunctions in action:

I. SIMPLE or GENERAL

A. Present

   si hoc facis, te prohibeo.
   If you do this, I stop you.

B. Past

   si hoc faciebas, te prohibebam.
   If [ever] you were doing this, I was [always] stopping you.
   si hoc fecisti, te prohibui.
   If you did this, I stopped you.

II. CONTRARY-TO-FACT or CONTRAFACTUAL or UNREAL

A. Present

   si hoc faceres, te prohiberem.
   If you were [right now] doing this [but you aren't], I would stop you.

B. Past

   si hoc fecisses, te prohibuissem.
   If you had done this [but you didn't], I would have stopped you.

III. FUTURE

A. More vivid

   si hoc facies, te prohibebo.
   If you do this, I will stop you.[2]

B. Less vivid

   si hoc facias, te prohibeam.
   If you should/were to do this, I would stop you.[3]

IV. MIXED: e.g.,

si hoc facies, te prohibeam.
   If you do this, I would stop you.
   PROTASIS: future more vivid; APODOSIS: future less vivid

si hoc faciebas, te prohibeo.
   If you used to do this thing [before], I stop you [from doing it now].
   PROTASIS: past simple; APODOSIS: present simple

si hoc facis, te prohibebo.
   If you ever do this, I will stop you.
   PROTASIS: present general; APODOSIS: future more vivid

---

2. If the contingency must emphatically be fulfilled for the consequence to occur, a future perfect indicative may be used in the protasis:

   si hoc feceris, te prohibebo.
   If, and only if, you do [i.e., will have done] this, will I stop you.

   In some old grammars, this is sometimes referred to as the future most vivid condition.

3. If the contingency must emphatically be fulfilled for the consequence to occur, a perfect subjunctive may be used in the protasis:

   si hoc feceris, te prohibeam.
   If, and only if, you should/were to do [i.e., have done] this, would I stop you.

   As we've seen, Latin can be rather punctilious about what action preceded another.

The following represents a tabular summary of the syntactical information about Latin conditionals:

TYPE	TIME	PROTASIS		APODOSIS	
		Tense	*Mood*	*Tense*	*Mood*
Simple/ General	Present	Present	Indicative	Present	Indicative
	Past	Imperfect, Perfect, Pluperfect	Indicative	Imperfect, Perfect, Pluperfect	Indicative
Future More Vivid	Future	Future/ Future Perfect	Indicative	Future	Indicative
Future Less Vivid	Future	Present/ Perfect	Subjunctive	Present	Subjunctive
Contrary-to-Fact	Present	Imperfect	Subjunctive	Imperfect	Subjunctive
	Past	Pluperfect	Subjunctive	Pluperfect	Subjunctive
Mixed		[any of the above, true to its own particular type]		[any of the above, true to its own particular type]	
NEGATION:		*nisi, si non*		*non*	

18. CONCESSIVE CLAUSES

We should mention an important subcategory of conditionals called **concessive clauses**. In English, concessive clauses are commonly introduced by the conjunctions 'although', 'though', 'even though', 'even if'; a coordinating sentence adverb like 'however', 'nonetheless', 'nevertheless', 'even so' can often be found in the main clause but only when the concessive clause precedes the main clause.

Concessive clauses can be understood as the protasis of a conditional sentence where the apodosis will be fulfilled regardless of whether or not the protasis is true.

> Even if/although Caesar is ill, we will leave.

In this sentence the speakers will leave irrespective of Caesar's current health status. Contrast the conditional:

> If Caesar is ill, we will leave.

In this sentence, the truth of the speakers' departure is conditioned entirely on Caesar's ill health. Presumably, if Caesar is not ill, the speakers will stay.

Remember, however, that where concessive clauses are used, the main clauses do not always or necessarily behave like the apodosis of conditional sentences.

In Latin, the conditional nature of concessive clauses is revealed by the conjunctions and the syntax used: some conjunctions "trigger" a subjunctive clause, implying a higher degree of contingency, while a different set of conjunctions is only used with the indicative mood, implying greater vividness.

18.1 *CUM*-CLAUSES

As we will see, *cum*-clauses are used in a variety of semantic contexts.[1] In concessive clauses, *cum* is always accompanied by a verb in the subjunctive; the verb in the main clause is often accompanied by the word *tamen* 'nevertheless',

---

1. The conjunction *cum*, derived from archaic Latin *quom*, should not be confused with the preposition *cum*.

'still' to make the concessiveness of the *cum*-clause explicit. The complete rules for the sequence of tenses (see §11.7.3) are at work here.

cum hoc facias, nos tamen sumus laeti. [PRIMARY SEQUENCE]
   Although you do this, we are still happy.

cum hoc feceris, nos tamen sumus laeti. [PRIMARY SEQUENCE]
   Although you have done this, we are still happy.

cum hoc faceres, nos tamen eramus laeti. [SECONDARY SEQUENCE]
   Although you were doing this, we were still happy.

cum hoc fecisses, nos tamen eramus laeti. [SECONDARY SEQUENCE]
   Although you had done this, we were still happy.

If the author or speaker wants to emphasize a notion of futurity, a future periphrastic (see §15.3) can be introduced with the subjunctive:

cum hoc facturus sis, nos tamen erimus.
   Although you are going to do this, we will still be happy.

18.2 CLAUSES WITH *QUAMVIS*

When *quamvis* is used as a conjunction, it generally introduces a subjunctive concessive clause. Again, the presence of the word *tamen* in the main clause underscores that the dependent clause is concessive.

quamvis hoc facias, nos tamen sumus.
   Although you do this, we are still happy.

18.3 INDICATIVE CLAUSES

The following conjunctions are generally used in indicative concessive clauses: *quamquam* 'although'; *etsi* 'even if', 'although'; *etiamsi* 'even if'; *tametsi* 'even if', 'even though'. A *tamen* may be present or absent from the main clause.

quamquam hoc facis, nos tamen sumus.
   Although you do this, we are still happy.

etiamsi hoc faciebas, nos tamen eramus.
Even if you were doing this, we were still happy.

All of the preceding types of concessive clauses are negated by *non*.

18.4 CLAUSES OF PROVISO

The conjunctions *dum, modo,* and *dummodo* (all meaning 'provided that', 'so long as', or 'if only') are used to express concessive wishes with present and imperfect subjunctives. The negative used in this special class of concessive clauses is *ne*.

veniant dum/modo/dummodo ne sint hostes.
Let them come, so long as they are not enemies.

benignus erat dum/modo/dummodo sibi placeret.
He was kind, provided that it pleased him.

tantum ut (negative: *tantum ne*) can also be used in proviso clauses:

veniant tantum ne sint hostes.
Let them come, so long as they are not enemies.

If futurity in a proviso clause is being emphasized, the subjunctive future periphrastic is exploited:

nunc discedant dum cras reventuri sint.
Let them depart now, so long as they will return tomorrow.

An alternate (and simpler) way of expressing concessive clauses is with participles (whether in ablative absolutes or not). See §§13 and 14.

19. RELATIVE CLAUSES

A **relative clause** is a subordinate clause that is introduced by a relative pronoun (see §§8.4, 9.2) or a relative adverb (see below). The English relative pronouns are 'who', 'whom', 'whose', 'which', 'what', 'that', 'who(so)ever', 'whom(so)ever', 'which(so)ever', and 'what(so)ever'. Some of these, like the personal pronouns, are marked for case (subjective, objective, possessive) and gender (masculine/ feminine, neuter):

who: subjective, masculine/feminine, singular and plural

whom: objective, masculine/feminine, singular and plural

whose: possessive, masculine/feminine and neuter, singular and plural

which: subjective and objective, neuter, singular and plural

The pronoun 'that' can be singular or plural, masculine/feminine or neuter, subjective or objective. 'What' stands in for 'that which' and is always neuter:

I don't agree with <u>what</u> you say. = I don't agree with <u>that</u> (thing) <u>which</u> you say.

Syntactically, relative clauses can function as either adjectival phrases or noun phrases. In the former case, the noun that the clause modifies is called its **antecedent**. In theory, the relative pronoun must agree with this antecedent in number and gender, but owing to its very limited declension, in practice this is an issue in only a few instances:

Fabius devised a <u>strategy</u> <u>which</u> (not <u>who</u>) led to victory. [NEUTER]

We need a <u>leader</u> <u>who</u> (not <u>which</u>) can inspire the people.
[MASCULINE/FEMININE]

The substitution of 'that' for 'who' or 'which' eliminates even this gender distinction:

Fabius devised a <u>strategy</u> <u>that</u> led to victory.

We need a <u>leader</u> <u>that</u> can inspire the people.

Although the relative pronouns do not show a morphological distinction between singular and plural, their number may become relevant if they serve as the subject of the verb in their clause:

I don't trust a <u>person who</u> always <u>agrees</u> with me. ['who' is singular]

I don't trust <u>people who</u> always <u>agree</u> with me. ['who' is plural]

If the relative pronoun serves some other function in its clause besides the subject, it is this function that determines its case:

The man <u>who loves the city</u> wins great praise. ['who' is the subject of 'loves']

The man <u>whom the city loves</u> wins great praise. ['whom' is the object of 'loves']

The man <u>whose city is rich</u> is never poor. ['whose' is a possessive, with 'city']

Relative pronouns in the objective case are sometimes omitted in less formal writing or speech, if this can be done without awkwardness or ambiguity:

The man the city loves wins great praise.

There are two ways an adjectival relative clause can modify its antecedent. A so-called **nonrestrictive** clause simply adds further information about the antecedent, and its deletion would not affect the validity of the sentence:

<u>Cato</u>, <u>who was a Roman senator</u>, wrote histories.

A **restrictive** clause, on the other hand, places a limit on the range of its antecedent, and its deletion would often result in an overly broad statement that thereby becomes invalid. In the English system of punctuation, it is generally not set off by commas:

<u>Roman generals</u> <u>who were also senators</u> were very common.

When the antecedent of the relative pronoun is indefinite ('he who', 'anyone who'), it can be omitted, though the result is often not very idiomatic:

He who laughs last, laughs best. → Who laughs last, laughs best.

More idiomatic is to replace the simple relative with the indefinite forms 'whoever', 'whomever', 'whatever', 'whichever'. The resulting clause functions as a noun rather than an adjective:

Whoever says this is lying. ['whoever says this' is the subject of 'is']

Whatever happens in Baiae stays in Baiae. ['whatever happens in Baiae' is the subject of 'stays']

I trust whomever you trust. ['whomever you trust' is the object of 'trust']

The pronouns 'which' and 'what' can sometimes refer to an entire clause as their antecedent:

He announced that the army had been victorious, which made everyone rejoice.

Finally, clauses headed by relative adverbs function adverbially:

When(ever) it rains, it pours.

Where(ever) there is smoke, there is fire.

There's no reason why this should happen.

How(ever) you answer this will decide your fate.

The indefinite adverbs are noted here with the suffix -ever added parenthetically.

The basic grammatical principles governing the English relative clause are essentially the same in Latin. The difference is that such clauses are far more frequent in Latin, and they show a far greater range of syntactic uses.

Because the Latin relative pronoun is fully inflected, the rules governing agreement and case are transparent: the pronoun will regularly take the gender and number of its antecedent, and its case will be determined by its grammatical function within its clause.

imperator qui Parthos vicit magnopere laudabatur.
The commander who defeated the Parthians was greatly praised.

imperator quem Parthi vicerunt magnopere reprehendebatur.
The commander whom the Parthians defeated was greatly reviled.

feminae quarum mariti pugnant multum patiuntur.
The women whose husbands are fighting suffer much.

feminae quibus nuntius victoriam nuntiavit gaudebant.
The women, to whom the messenger announced the victory, rejoiced.

Like all adverbs, relative adverbs are indeclinable:

qua cives deos non verentur, iustitia marcet.
Where the citizens do not fear the gods, justice withers.

The relative can serve to link two sentences together, in which case it is often better translated with a personal pronoun:

quis illi oratori credat? qui populum saepe decipit.
Who would trust that speaker? He often deceives the people.

Corresponding to the English 'which' or 'what', the neuter relative pronoun can have an entire clause as its antecedent, although in Latin the relative clause often comes first:

quod esse ridiculissimum nobis videbatur, equus saltare coepit.
What seemed most ridiculous to us, the horse began to dance.

The rule governing the case of the relative pronoun is occasionally violated by the phenomenon of **attraction**, where the pronoun is "attracted" into the case of its antecedent:

cum fratre meo quo cognovisti veniam. [*quo* rather than *quem*]
I'll be coming with my brother, whom you know.

Rarely, you may also encounter an example of reverse attraction, where the antecedent is attracted to the case of the relative pronoun, as determined by its function in its clause. To link the antecedent and relative pronoun even more closely, the antecedent may be incorporated into the relative clause itself and take on the case of the pronoun:

ubi inveniemus qui homo nos servabit?
Where will we find a man who will save us?

rather than

ubi inveniemus hominem qui nos servabit?

19.1 FINE POINTS

Far beyond their potential in English, Latin relative clauses can encompass many other syntactic functions. In many cases it is not possible to retain the relative structure in an idiomatic English translation.

(1) Imperative.   *epistulam tibi mittam quam diligenter lege.*
I will send you a letter. Read it carefully.

(2) Wish.   *optimates odi quos utinam dei deleant!*
I hate the aristocrats. May the gods destroy them!

(3) **Relative and adverbial clauses of purpose** (see §20) are introduced by words having antecedents in the main clause and generally take the subjunctive in Latin. The introductory word can be either a relative pronoun:

ego legatum mitto qui reginam interroget.
I am sending a legate [in order] to question the queen.

vilicus ancillam invenit quae dominam curaret.
The bailiff found a slave girl to care for the mistress.

or an adverb of place or location, like *ubi* 'where', *unde* 'from where', or *quo* '[to] where':

ego ad triclinium contendo ubi cenam inveniam.
I am hurrying to the dining room where I may find dinner.
I am hurrying to the dining room to find dinner there.

captivi carcerem deploraverunt unde effugerent.
The captives complained about the prison to escape from there.

In a very specialized use of this construction, the word *quo* (ablative, 'by which [act]') introduces a purpose clause containing a comparative:

nos de via adgrediebamur quo melius pompam aspectaremus.
We were advancing down the street to watch the parade better.

imperator ad Galliam proficiscitur quo maiores equos inveniat.
The commander is setting out for Gaul to find bigger horses.

(4) The same relative pronouns and relative adverbs discussed above for purpose clauses can also be used for subjunctive result clauses (see §21):

nullus imperator est tam stultus qui Romanos non timeat.
No commander is so foolish as to not fear Romans.

tantam tabernam emit quo plures emptores adliceret.

He bought such a big shop <u>that</u> he <u>attracted</u> more customers.

(5) Conditions. A relative clause can function as the protasis of any type of condition; the mood and tense of its verb will follow the general rules governing conditional sentences of that particular type (for which see §17). For example, the verb in a relative clause functioning as the protasis of a simple/general condition will be in some tense of indicative, as established by logic and the tense of the main verb:

quocumque ire vis, sequimur. [= *si quo ire vis, sequimur*]

<u>Wherever</u> you wish to go, we follow.

quem esse mortuum cupivisti, necavimus. [= *si quem . . .*]

<u>Whomever</u> you wanted dead, we murdered.

(6) **Relative clauses of characteristic** (also called **generic relative clauses**). Certain dependent subjunctive clauses are introduced by a form (usually in the nominative) of the relative pronoun (*qui, quae, quod,* etc.). These clauses describe their antecedent in some indefinite property or characteristic relative to a larger, specified group or class to which the antecedent belongs.

est homo qui cito exeat.

He is the (sort of) person who exits fast.

He is a person who exits fast.

He is the (sort of) person to exit fast.

(Notice that the person is described in terms of relation to a broader group of which he is just one member. Contrast:

est homo qui cito exit.

He is <u>the</u> (actual) person who exits fast.

In this sentence the relative clause defines something specific, not generic.)

The most common introductory phrases for this construction are the following:

sunt/erant qui: there are/were those who

est/erat qui: he is/was one/the sort who

nemo est/erit qui: there is/will be no one who

solus est/erat qui: he is/was the only one who

nihil est/erat quod: there is/was nothing which

quis est/erit qui?: who is there/will there be who?

quid est/erat quod?: what is/was there that?

Negative relative clauses of characteristic are commonly introduced by *quin* (= *qui* [*quae, quod*] *ne*):

> *nemo est quin hoc negaverit.*
> There is no one who did not deny this.

Finally, if futurity in a generic clause is being emphasized, the subjunctive future periphrastic is used (see §15.3.1):

> *estis soli qui cras recepturi sitis.*
> You alone are the sorts to retreat tomorrow.

20. PURPOSE CLAUSES

Purpose clauses (also known as **final clauses**) answer the question 'to what end?' or 'for what effect?' the action of the main verb is performed. In English, the minimal structure of a purpose clause looks like this:

He rose <u>to</u> greet me.[1]

But because purpose is necessary to the action, this is only a truncation of the more expansive:

He rose <u>in order to</u> greet me *or*

He rose <u>so to</u> greet me.[2]

And for these there are two conjunctive alternatives:

He rose <u>in order that</u> he might greet me.

He rose <u>so that</u> he might greet me.

When the subject of the subordinate clause differs from the subject of the main verb, English offers these options:

He sent them <u>to</u> greet me.

He sent them <u>in order to</u> greet me.[3]

He sent them <u>in order that</u> they might greet me.

He sent them <u>so that</u> they might greet me.

He sent them <u>that</u> they might greet me.

In formal English, when the main verb is in the present, future, or present perfect tense, the auxiliary verb 'may' is required in the purpose clause; when

---

1. Be careful not to confuse purpose clauses with complementary infinitives (e.g., 'he desires to greet me'), which typically express need, effort, or intention.
2. Consider the archaic and poetic: He rose <u>for to</u> greet me.
3. Observe the ambiguity in the English sentences: 'He sent them to annoy me' and 'He sent them in order to annoy me'. Who, presumably, is doing the annoying? Latin doesn't exhibit a similar ambiguity.

the main verb is in any of the other past tenses, the auxiliary verb 'might' is required in the purpose clause:

> She sends us in order that we <u>may</u> greet them.
>
> She has sent us so that we <u>may</u> greet them.
>
> She was sending us in order that we <u>might</u> greet them.
>
> She had sent us so that we <u>might</u> greet them.

In the English of common, everyday usage, however, these auxiliaries are usually omitted.

Latin also has several alternatives for expressing the notion of purpose. We've seen future participles used to this end (see §13.1.(2)), accusative supines (see §15.1.(1)), gerunds and gerundives with the preposition *ad* or the postpositions *causa* and *gratia* (see §15.2), and even (rarely) infinitives (see §12). In the previous chapter, we learned that relative clauses can express purpose, too (see §19.1.(3)). Consider,

> They come in order to listen.
>
> *audituri veniunt.*
>
> *auditum veniunt.*
>
> *ad audiendum veniunt.*
>
> *audiendi gratia/causa veniunt.*
>
> *audire veniunt.*
>
> *qui audiant veniunt.*

20.1 WITH *UT* OR *NE*

The more common construction, though, involves a subordinate clause introduced by the Latin final conjunction *ut*. Purpose clauses are negated by substituting the *ut* with *ne*.[4]

---

4. Now obsolescent except in "frozen phrases" like 'lest we forget', the English conjunction 'lest' means 'so that not' or 'in order that not'. It can often be found in older translations but it is quite rare in modern American speech.

The syntax of Latin purpose clauses is fairly straightforward: if the main verb is in a primary tense (i.e., present, future, present perfect, or future perfect), the subordinate verb is in the present subjunctive; but if the main verb is in a secondary tense (i.e., imperfect, aoristic perfect, or pluperfect), the subordinate verb will be in the imperfect subjunctive.

> *ut audiant veniunt.*
>> They come in order to listen.

> *ut audirent veniebant.*
>> They were coming in order to listen.

> *ne audiant veniunt.*
>> They come that they may not listen.

> *ne audirent veniebant.*
>> They were coming that they might not listen.

20.2 CLAUSES OF PREVENTION

Closely akin to purpose clauses are **clauses of prevention**. The following verbs usually take a subjunctive construction:

> *deterreo, -ere, deterrui, deterritus:* deter, prevent
>
> *impedio, ire, impedivi (impedii), impeditus:* hinder
>
> *interdico, -ere, interdixi, interdictus:* ban
>
> *moror, -ari, moratus sum:* deter, hinder
>
> *obsisto, -ere, obstiti, obstitus:* resist, stand in the way of
>
> *obsto, -are, obstiti, obstatus:* hinder, stand in the way of
>
> *officio, -ere, offeci, offectus:* hinder, obstruct

For affirmed prevention, the subjunctive is introduced by the conjunctions *quominus* or *ne:*

> *deterreo quominus discedas:* I prevent you from departing.
>
> *impedio ne discedas:* I hinder you from departing.

For negated prevention, the subjunctive is introduced by *quominus* or *quin:*

> *non deterreo quin discedas:* I don't prevent you from departing.
>
> *non impedivi quominus discederes:* I didn't hinder your departing.[5]

20.3 INDIRECT COMMANDS

See §16.3 for **indirect commands**, which are related to purpose clauses.

---

5. The verbs *prohibeo, -ere, prohibui, prohibitus* 'prohibit'; *tardo, -are, tardavi, tardatus* 'detain from'; and *veto, -are, vetui, vetitus* 'forbid' usually take simple complementary infinitives:

> *te veto discedere:* I forbid you to depart.
> *te prohibeo discedere:* I prohibit you from departing.

The verb *prohibeo* can, however, be found with a dependent verb in the subjunctive.

21. RESULT CLAUSES

Result clauses (also known as **consecutive clauses**) are subordinate clauses that answer the question 'to what extent?' or 'to what degree?' was the action or condition of the main verb carried to an outcome. Thus, the stated result is necessary to complete the sense of the main clause.

He is so unhappy that he doesn't eat.

She became such a good speaker that everyone respected her.

We caught so many fish that we reached the limit within an hour.

They acted in such a way as to confuse us.

I will complain so much to the owner as to get my money back.

With these examples, you'll notice that the first three sentences represent real or actual results, while the latter two sentences represent expected or potential results. You'll also notice that the result clauses are triggered by the adverbs 'so' and 'such', which help distinguish result clauses from purpose clauses (see §20):

They acted this way (so) to confuse us. [PURPOSE]

They acted in such a way as to confuse us. [RESULT]

She became a good speaker in order that everyone might respect her. [PURPOSE]

She became such a good speaker that everyone respected her. [RESULT]

Latin uses the consecutive conjunction *ut* to introduce all result clauses. In the main clauses of result constructions the following trigger words are often found:

ADJECTIVES: *tantus, -a, -um:* so great
     talis, -e: such, of such a kind
     tot [indeclinable]: so many

ADVERBS: *ita* [usually used with verbs]: so
     sic [usually with verbs]: in such a way
     totiens [usually with verbs]: so often
     tantum [usually with verbs]: so much
     tam [usually with adverbs and adjectives]: so
     adeo [usually with adverbs and adjectives]: so

Latin makes no morphological distinction between real or factual results and potential or intended results. All result clauses are simply put in the subjunctive. The tense of the subjunctive is determined, as we saw above for purpose clauses, by the tense of the main verb: if the main verb is in a primary tense (i.e., present, future, present perfect, or future perfect), the subordinate verb is in the present subjunctive; but if the main verb is in a secondary tense (i.e., imperfect, aoristic perfect, or pluperfect), the subordinate verb will be in the imperfect subjunctive.

> *sic se gerunt ut nos perturbent.*
> They act in such a way as to confuse us.

> *tam bona orator facta est ut omnes eam observarent.*
> She became such a good speaker that everyone respected her.

Result clauses are negated with *ut non.*

> *sic se gerunt ut nos non perturbent.*
> They act in such a way as not to confuse us.

> *Tam bona orator facta est ut nemo eam non observaret.*
> She became such a good speaker that no one didn't respect her.

22. OBJECT CLAUSES

So far, we have seen that some verbs can employ a noun (the direct object) to complete their meaning and others a nonfinite verb phrase containing either an infinitive or, less often, a participle. For certain types of verbs it is a subordinate clause that plays this role, appropriately called an **object clause**.

In English, these clauses are generally introduced by the conjunction 'that':

I fear <u>that the worst will happen</u>.

Take care <u>that the children come to no harm</u>.

They saw to it <u>that the people learned the truth</u>.

An alternative conjunction, the archaic 'lest', can be substituted in some contexts (with the subjunctive):

I fear <u>lest the worst happen</u>.

Take care <u>lest the children come to harm</u>.

In Latin, there are two classes of verbs that commonly govern object clauses in the subjunctive.

22.1 VERBS OF EFFORT

This category includes verbs like *efficere* 'bring it about that', 'make sure that', *curare* 'take care that', *operam dare* 'pay attention that', and the like. The object clauses are usually introduced by *ut,* and the subordinate verb is most commonly in the subjunctive, in both primary and secondary sequences. The negative is usually *ut non*.

> *efficite ut <u>rex hanc epistulam accipiat</u>.*
> Make sure <u>that the king receives this letter</u>.

> *Sinon operam dedit ut <u>Troes non suspicarentur</u>.*
> Sinon paid attention <u>that the Trojans would not be suspicious</u>.

22.2 VERBS OF FEARING

Verbs or expressions of fearing take subjunctive clauses introduced by *ne* for the positive and *ut* for the negative. While this may seem a curious reversal, it is the result of a logical development of the language. In the earliest period of Latin, the construction was paratactic (**parataxis** is the absence of grammatical subordination); and the sentences were simple and consecutive:

> *timeo. ut veniat!:* I am afraid. If only he would come!

> *timeo. ne veniat!:* I am afraid. If only he would not come!

In these sentences, *veniat* is an optative subjunctive; thus, in parataxis, the fear was simply asserted and a related desire expressed.

As Latin developed, the construction became hypotactic (**hypotaxis** is the subordination of one clause to another; sentences become complex and composed of one or more dependent clause):

> *timeo ut veniat:* I am afraid that he is not coming.

> *timeo ne veniat:* I am afraid that he is coming.

Thus, in hypotaxis, the assertion of fear and the expressed desire were combined; it is logical that the objects of one's fears and wishes would be opposites.

Clauses of fearing follow the normal rule for sequence of tenses (see §11.7.3):

> *timeo ut veniat:* I am afraid that he is not coming.

> *timeo ut venerit:* I am afraid that he has not come.

> *timebam ut veniret:* I was afraid that he was not coming.

> *timebam ut venisset:* I was afraid that he had not come.

The future periphrastic (the future participle plus the verb 'to be') is used to express futurity with emphasis:

> *timeo ut venturus sit:* I am afraid that he will not come.

> *timebam ut venturus esset:* I was afraid that he would not come.

Sometimes *ne . . . non* (a double negative) is used instead of *ut* to express a negative clause of fearing:

> *timeo ne non veniat:* I am afraid that he is not coming.

22.3 WITH INFINITIVES

Rarely, an object clause can be expressed with an infinitive:

nihil certum habes, ne <u>amare</u> quidem aut <u>amari</u>.

You grasp nothing for certain, not even <u>to love</u> or <u>to be loved</u>.

23. CAUSAL CLAUSES

A **causal clause** is a subordinate clause that answers the question 'why?' the main clause occurred. In English, subordinate clauses are typically introduced by the conjunctions 'since', 'because', and 'as'.

Because Nero has died, the empire is in confusion.

We will head to the forum now since an assembly will be convened soon.

As I'm not feeling very well, I'm going to bed.

In Latin, causal clauses are introduced by a variety of different conjunctions, each requiring its own specific syntax. In some cases, the mood of the verb and the conjunction used will help you determine whether the causal clause in Latin is factual, on the one hand, or alleged, assumed, contrafactual, or potential, on the other.

23.1 *CUM*-CLAUSES

The conjunction *cum* (from archaic Latin *quom* and distinct from the preposition *cum*), meaning 'because' or 'since', takes the subjunctive and follows the sequence of tenses (see §11.7.3):

cum fortiter pugnemus, hostes nostros vincimus.
Since we are fighting bravely, we are defeating our enemy.

cum dormirent, impetum fecimus.
Since they were sleeping, we made an attack.

The "language logic" of the subjunctive here is the implied contingency: if the causal clause weren't true, perhaps the main clause would not be true.

23.2 WITH *QUONIAM* AND *QUANDO*

The conjunctions *quoniam* and *quando* 'since', 'because' are used mostly with the indicative:

I help because you are in danger.
quando/quoniam perclitamini iuvo.

I helped because you were in danger.
quando/quoniam perclitabamini iuvi.

23.3 CONJUNCTIONS WITH EITHER THE SUBJUNCTIVE OR THE INDICATIVE

Certain conjunctions can take either the indicative or the subjunctive depending largely on the implication of the sentence and revealing the author's or speaker's bias. The conjunctions *quod*, *quia*, and *quippe* (usually followed by *qui*), all meaning 'because' or 'since', are used in this way. Remember: the indicative is the mood of fact, while the subjunctive is the mood of assumption, intention, or probability. When the causal clause is factual, the indicative is used; when it is assumed, alleged, or intended, the subjunctive is used:

> *nos sollicitant quod/quia/quippe qui veniunt.*
> They worry us because they are [actually] coming.

> *nos sollicitant quod/quia/quippe qui veniant.*
> They worry us because they are [allegedly] coming/because they may/ could come.

If the futurity of the causal clause is assumed, alleged, or intended, a future periphrastic with the subjunctive should be used:

> *nos sollicitant quod/quia/quippe qui venturi sint.*
> They worry us because they will [allegedly] come.

Two alternate methods for expressing causals are quite common. As we've seen in §§13 and 14, participles (whether in an ablative absolute or not) frequently are used causally. Moreover, a gerund or gerundive (see §15) in the accusative after the prepositions *ob* or *propter* expresses causation.

> *vobis perclitantibus, arma cepit.*

> *ob/propter vos perclitandos, arma cepit.*
> Because of your being in danger, he took up arms.

24. TEMPORAL CLAUSES

From a practical standpoint, defining time with some specificity is one of the most important tasks a language must perform: what happens when, what occurs before what, what transpires after what, and what things take place roughly at the same time. The importance of time has already been observed for prepositions, adverbs, conjunctions, and the tenses of verbs. We see it, too, with participles, absolute phrases, conditionals, and indirect statement. An inference can be drawn here: language recognizes a great need for pinpointing time, especially when one event takes place in a context with one or more other events.

In this chapter, we examine **temporal clauses**, that is, subordinate clauses within complex sentences, where the relationship between the main clauses and the dependent clauses is established by means of a time referent. This time referent is usually a subordinating conjunction (see §28.2) that specifies whether the action of the dependent clause is prior to, subsequent to, or roughly simultaneous with the action of the main clause.

Before email was invented, there were only the telephone and letters. [SUBSEQUENT]

I will hold this memory dear until the day I die. [SUBSEQUENT]

After we left, the hurricane hit. [PRIOR]

The hurricane hit as soon as we left. [PRIOR]

Ever since they won, they've been really arrogant. [PRIOR]

When you arrive, it will be my birthday. [SIMULTANEOUS]

I sacrificed to the gods so long as I was successful. [SIMULTANEOUS]

While we were sleeping, the enemy attacked. [SIMULTANEOUS]

For temporal clauses, English relies semantically more on the subordinating conjunctions than on the tenses of its verbs:

I will wait to do this until you leave.

I will wait to do this until you have left.

I will wait to do this until you will have left.

Notice how there really isn't a significant difference in meaning between these three sentences, despite the changes in tense in the subordinate clauses.

In Latin, too, there's considerable importance given to the subordinating conjunctions and the mood(s) that typically accompany them. The variety here is impressive. All of the following are negated with *non* (unless some other ambient grammar requires *ne*). Also, all of the following can theoretically occur in future periphrastics, if in fact futurity is being emphasized.

24.1 CUM-CLAUSES

There are several types of temporal *cum*-clauses and they each behave somewhat differently.

(1) If the *cum*-clause refers strictly to time and its action is coordinate with the action of the main verb (i.e., if the *cum*-clause merely fixes the time of the action of the main verb), this is a true **temporal *cum*-clause** and its verb is in the indicative:

> *cum venietis, erit meus dies natalis.*
>
> [At the very time] when you [will] come, it will be my birthday.
>
> *cum Scipio discessit, regina moriebatur.*
>
> [At the very time] when Scipio departed, the queen was dying.

(2) If the *cum*-clause states the circumstances in which the action of the main verb takes place, this is a **circumstantial *cum*-clause**. If the action of the circumstantial clause is in the present or future time, the present or future indicative is used:

> *cum nos fiemus senes, erimus divites.*
>
> When we [will] become old men, we will be rich.
>
> *cum ego te video, laetus sum.*
>
> When I see you, I am happy.

If the action of the circumstantial clause is in the past time, the imperfect or pluperfect subjunctive is used:

> *cum villam incendissetis, discessistis.*
>
> When/After you had set fire to the house, you departed.
>
> *cum milites dormirent, centurio epistulas scripsit.*
>
> When/While the soldiers were sleeping, the centurion wrote letters.

Distinguishing between temporal and circumstantial only requires you to ask this question: would the statement of the main clause still have been true regardless of the *cum*-clause? If so, it is a temporal clause. If not, it is a circumstantial clause.

(3) When the *cum*-clause conveys a generalization, the conjunction is translated 'whenever'. This is called a **generalizing *cum*-clause**. The perfect indicative is used to make a present generalization:

> *cum vos vidimus, laeti sumus.*
> Whenever we see [literally, have seen] you, we are happy.

The pluperfect indicative is used to make a past generalization:

> *cum vos videramus, laeti eramus.*
> Whenever we saw [literally, had seen] you, we were happy.

The tense of the *cum*-clause (perfect or pluperfect) specifies that the action of the generalization was prior to the action of the main verb.

24.2 CONSTRUCTIONS WITH INDICATIVE

Certain common temporal conjunctions are used only with the indicative mood:

cum primum: as soon as

postquam: after

quando: when

simul ac or *simulac:* as soon as

simul atque or *simulatque:* as soon as

ubi: when, after, while

ut: when, as, while

It was night when he came.
> *nox erat quando venit.*

After he came, we sacrificed.
> *postquam venit, sacrificavimus.*

We did this <u>as soon as</u> he came.
hoc fecimus <u>cum primum</u> venit.

We do this <u>as soon as</u> he comes.
hoc facimus <u>simul ac</u> venit.

We do this <u>while</u> he comes.
hoc facimus <u>ut</u> venit.

24.3 CONSTRUCTIONS WITH INDICATIVE OR SUBJUNCTIVE

Other common temporal conjunctions take either indicative or subjunctive depending largely on the implication of the sentence or to reveal the author's or speaker's bias: *dum* 'until', 'as long as', 'while'; *donec* 'until', 'as long as', 'while'; *quoad* 'until', 'as long as', 'while'. Again, remember: the indicative is the mood of fact, while the subjunctive is the mood of assumption, intention, or probability. When these refer merely to a temporal idea, they take the indicative:

exspectabamus <u>dum/donec/quoad</u> venisti.
We waited <u>until</u> you [actually] came.

exspectabamus <u>dum/donec/quoad</u> volui.
We waited <u>as long as</u> I wanted.

exspectabamus <u>dum/donec/quoad</u> locuti sunt.
We waited <u>while/until</u> they spoke.

dum normally takes the present indicative (the so-called historical present) to denote continued action in the past time:

<u>dum</u> officinam <u>habeo</u>, maritus mortuus est.
<u>While</u> I <u>had</u> my shop, my husband died.

When the notion of purpose, intention, or futurity is involved, the subjunctive is used:

exspectabamus <u>dum/donec/quoad</u> venires.
We waited <u>until</u> you should come.
We waited <u>for</u> you to come.

(Notice that the sentence does <u>not</u> indicate whether the person did in fact come.)

exspectabamus <u>dum/donec/quoad</u> locuti essent.
We waited <u>until</u> <u>they would have spoken</u>.
We waited <u>for</u> <u>them to have spoken</u>.

(Again, notice that the sentence doesn't indicate whether the persons did in fact speak.)

24.4 WITH *ANTEQUAM* AND *PRIUSQUAM*

Two other conjunctions may take either the subjunctive or the indicative mood: *antequam* and *priusquam*, both meaning 'before'. When these refer strictly to time, they take the indicative:

discessit <u>priusquam/antequam</u> <u>veni</u>.
She left <u>before</u> <u>I came</u>.

When purpose, intention, or assumption is involved, the subjunctive is used in secondary sequence:

discessit <u>priusquam/antequam</u> <u>venirem</u>.
She left <u>before</u> <u>I might/could come</u>.

In primary sequence, the present or future perfect <u>indicative</u> is generally used (less frequently, the present subjunctive):

discedet <u>priusquam/antequam</u> <u>venero</u>.
She will leave <u>before</u> <u>I will have come</u>.

discedet <u>priusquam</u> <u>venio/veniam</u>.
She will leave <u>before</u> <u>I come</u>.

Frequently *ante/quam* and *prius/quam* are split in a figure called tmesis (see §10):

<u>ante/prius</u> discessit <u>quam</u> venirem.
She left before [literally, sooner than] I could come.

You may find it helpful to study temporal clauses if their conjunctions are presented alphabetically in tabular form:

CONJUNCTION	MEANING(S)	MOOD OF TEMPORAL CLAUSE
antequam	before	factual: indicative
		assumed: subjunctive
cum (circumstantial)	when	pres./fut. circumstance: indicative
		past circumstance: subjunctive
cum (generalizing)	whenever	pres. generalization: perf. indicative
		past generalization: pluperf. indicative
cum (temporal)	when	indicative
cum primum	as soon as	indicative
donec	until, as long as, while	factual: indicative
		assumed: subjunctive
dum	until, as long as, while	factual: indicative (usu. present)
		assumed: subjunctive
postquam	after	indicative
priusquam	before	factual: indicative
		assumed: subjunctive
quando	when	indicative
quoad	until, as long as, while	factual: indicative
		assumed: subjunctive
simul ac or *simulac*	as soon as	indicative
simul atque or *simulatque*	as soon as	indicative
ubi	when, after, while	indicative
ut	when, as, while	indicative

25. INTERROGATIVE SENTENCES

Any English declarative sentence can be turned into a question with no syntactic alteration. In speaking, such a sentence is marked as interrogative by a rising voice inflection at the end; in writing, this is accomplished by a change in punctuation:

Seneca is the wisest man in Rome.

Seneca is the wisest man in Rome?

Most commonly, however, the change from a declarative to an interrogative sentence is marked by slight changes in syntax. If the main verb of the sentence is a form of the verb 'to be', interrogation is indicated by reversing the order of the subject and verb.

Seneca is the wisest man in Rome.

Is Seneca the wisest man in Rome?

Similarly, in a sentence with a compound verb (i.e., a verb augmented with an auxiliary), the order of the subject and the auxiliary verb is reversed:

Seneca has been put to death.

Has Seneca been put to death?

Finally, sentences with simple verbs are turned into questions through the use of the auxiliary verb 'do':

The Romans admire(d) wise men.

Do the Romans admire wise men?

Did the Romans admire wise men?

Questions that ask for other types of information besides yes-or-no answers are introduced by interrogative pronouns and adverbs placed at the beginning of the sentence. Interrogative pronouns are used exactly as personal pronouns would be:

Romans have put Seneca to death.

Who has put Seneca to death?

Questions introduced by interrogative adverbs involve the word order changes listed above:

> Why is Seneca the wisest man in Rome?
>
> Where has Seneca been put to death?
>
> How much do the Romans admire wise men?

Yes-or-no questions can be asked in such a way as to indicate that the speaker expects a particular answer:

> You are going to the festival, aren't you?
>
> You are not going to wear that, are you?

In Latin, the situation is actually less complex. Interrogative pronouns, adjectives, and adverbs are regularly placed at or near the beginning of the sentence, just as in English:

> *quis haec tibi dixit?*
>> Who told you this?
>
> *quo philosophi omnes ierunt?*
>> Where have all the philosophers gone?

Yes-or-no questions are commonly (but not necessarily) introduced with the enclitic interrogative particle *-ne.*

> *amasne illam mulierem?*
>> Do you love that woman?

Latin also allows the questioner to prejudice the answer, either as positive with the particle *nonne* or as negative with *num:*

> *nonne illam mulierem amas?*
>> Don't you love that woman?
>> You love that woman, don't you?
>
> *num illam mulierem amas?*
>> You don't love that woman, do you?

The particle *quin*, which is used with the subjunctive mood in various types of subordinate clause, is also used in main clauses with different senses. In interrogatives, the word means 'why not?', expressing emphasis or even an implicit command:

> *quin illam mulierem amas?*
> Why **don't** you love that woman?
> Why **not** love that woman?[1]

---

1. In declarative sentences and with imperatives, *quin* means 'but, rather':

   quin eam amat: But, rather, he loves her.
   quin eam ama!: But, rather, love her!

IV. SOME OTHER GRAMMATICAL ELEMENTS

26. ADVERBS

Adverbs have traditionally been defined as words that specifically modify adjectives, verbs, and other adverbs:

We <u>gladly</u> listened to Seneca. [MODIFYING A VERB]

This play is <u>deservedly</u> famous. [MODIFYING AN ADJECTIVE]

They fought <u>uncharacteristically</u> poorly. [MODIFYING AN ADVERB]

In modern English usage, however, adverbs can commonly be seen to modify entire clauses or sentences:

<u>Sadly</u>, Mr. Smith passed away yesterday.

<u>Hopefully</u>, it will rain tomorrow.

<u>Regrettably</u>, no one showed up.

<u>Interestingly</u>, they're all Canadians.

<u>Embarrassingly</u>, the chairs were already taken.

<u>Supposedly</u>, they're coming today.

These so-called sentence adverbs are typically placed first in their clause; if placed last in their clause, they come off as an apparent afterthought or sometimes as irony:

It will rain tomorrow, <u>hopefully</u>.

All the chairs were already taken, <u>embarrassingly</u>.

They're coming today, <u>supposedly</u>.

Most English adverbs express temporal or locative relations, manner, or degree:

You will arrive <u>later</u>. [TEMPORAL]

The people worship no gods <u>there</u>. [LOCATIVE]

They <u>easily</u> won. [MANNER]

This amount is <u>far</u> greater. [DEGREE]

An interesting feature of English usage, the use of adjectives with pronouns in the subjective case is sometimes felt to be awkward and is therefore replaced with the use of an adverb:

I, happy, went on my way.

Happy, I went on my way.

<u>Happily</u>, I went on my way.

This replacement in the objective case is not so simple:

He gave the book to happy me.

He gave the book to me, happy.

These two sentences seem quite awkward, but no adverbial replacement is available. Hence, some sort of grammatical expansion must be employed:

He gave the book to me, <u>and I was happy</u>.

He gave the book to me, <u>making me happy</u>.

He gave the book to me, <u>because I was happy</u>.

The functions and usage of the Latin adverb are comparable to the English.

Senecam <u>libenter</u> audiebamus.
   We <u>gladly</u> listened to Seneca.

haec fabula est <u>merito</u> clara.
   This play is <u>deservedly</u> famous.

<u>insolenter</u> male pugnaverunt.
   They fought <u>uncharacteristically</u> poorly.

<u>serius</u> pervenietis.
   You will arrive <u>later</u>.

ibi populus deos nullos veneratur.
> The people worship no gods there.

facile vicerunt.
> They easily won.

haec summa est multo maior.
> This amount is far greater.

26.1 FINE POINTS

Now that you've graduated from Latin Adverbs 101, let's look at some of the finer points of this Latin part of speech.

First, one could appropriately say that many of the Latin particles (see §27) serve as the structural and functional equivalents of sentence adverbs.

When nouns convey an adjectival or verbal sense or force, they occasionally can be modified by an adverb, especially in poetry:

puer admodum: quite a boy, fully a boy

fortiter facta: deeds bravely done

late rex: a king far and wide

Some locative and temporal adverbs are used with the ablative of separation (and other ablatives) and thus function as prepositions:

palam illis: in the presence of those

procul hoc: far from this

simul nobis: together with us

Some other locative and temporal adverbs are used with the accusative case and thus function as prepositions:

usque urbem: up to the city

postridie ludos: on the day after the games

proprius montem: nearer to the mountain

Some prepositions, for example, *ante, post, adversus, circiter,* and *prope,* are used without substantives and thus function as adverbs:

quod ante dixi: which I said before

nemo adversus ibat: nobody approached confrontationally

circiter hora quarta: at approximately the fourth hour

You should notice how many parts of speech can be translated adverbially into English:

prepositional phrases:
sine lege: without agreement → willy-nilly
per urbem: throughout the city → citywide

substantives in the ablative or accusative:
lege: with law → legally
partem: to an extent
nihil: not at all

participial phrases:
amans: being loving → lovingly

adjectival phrases:
merus et iustus: perfect and just → perfectly just

26.2 DEGREES OF COMPARISON

Like adjectives (see §6.2), many adverbs have three **degrees of comparison**: positive, comparative, and superlative. The most common ending for positive adverbs is *-e* and *-(i)ter* (like English '_____ly'); for comparatives, *-ius* (English 'more _____ly', 'rather _____ly'); and for superlatives *-issime* (English 'most _____ly', 'very _____ly').

Like English, some very common Latin adverbs exhibit irregular comparatives and superlatives built on different stems. As you will encounter these words often, it will be helpful to you to master them:

well: *bene, melius, optime (optume)*

badly, ill, poorly: *male, peius, pessime (pessume)*

greatly, mightily: *magnopere, magis (mage), maxime (maxume)*

slightly, a little: *parum, minus, minime (minume)*

much: *multum (multo), magis (mage), maxime (maxume)*

much: *multum (multo), plus, plurime (plurume)*

near: *prope, propius, proxime*

beyond, far: *ultra, ulterius, ultime*

Some common irregular adverbs that lack positive degrees are these:

badly, ill, poorly: *deterius, deterrime*

swiftly: *ocius, ocissime*

rather, especially: *potius, potissimum*

before, prior: *prius, primum*

27. PARTICLES

Particles, as we defined in §2.7, are little words (or non-words) that are added to a clause or sentence to contribute some nuance or cue that aids in the interpretation of that sentence or clause. For example,

I hate this game.

Arrgh, I hate this game.

In the first of these sentences, the listener or reader won't necessarily know why the speaker hates the game. In the second sentence, the presence of 'arrgh' communicates to the listener or reader that the speaker hates the game due to some frustration.

One way you can distinguish between a particle and an interjection is word position: generally, an interjection can be placed anywhere in its sentence or clause, while a particle can usually be placed in only one or two positions within its context:

Arrgh, I hate this game.

or

I hate this game, arrgh.

but not

I hate, arrgh, this game.

As we saw in the previous chapter, particles and sentence adverbs bear some functional similarities, as do sentence conjunctions and particles (see next chapter).

The most important thing to note about Latin particles is that they are common in all genres of literature. Placed, typically, as either the first or second word of their clause, they serve as a constant signal to readers how to interpret that clause. Because particles can be used in common combinations, one can find clauses or sentences where the first two or three words are all particles. Although some particles appear to us to be synonymous, to native speakers they conveyed subtle shades of difference and revealed idiolect (an individualistic preference or "default" of the speaker or writer). In translation, readers will sometimes opt not to translate a given particle, but they should *never* ignore the tone, coloration, or nuance that particles lend to the Latin language.

According to most formal grammar books, technically all adverbs, conjunctions, and interjections are particles. But not every particle is, for example, a conjunction (or an adverb, or an interjection). Thus, we have already encountered some particles in previous chapters.

Latin particles are typically classified as follows:

CONDITIONAL: *si* 'if'; *ni, nisi* 'unless'

INTERROGATIVE: *an, -ne, anne, utrum, utrumne, num* 'whether?'; *annon, nonne* 'whether not?'; *numquid, ecquid* 'whether at all?'; *quin* 'why not?'

NEGATIVE: *non, haud, haut, minime, ne* 'not'; *nec, neque, neve, neu* 'nor', 'neither'; *nedum* 'much less'; *ne* 'lest'; *ne . . . quidem* 'not even'; *quominus* 'so as not'; *quin* 'but that'.

Being a bit tricky, particles should be mastered with a special diligence, precisely because they are more important to Latin stylistics than they are to English.

28. CONJUNCTIONS

As we saw in §2.8, **conjunctions** are words that link grammatically equivalent words, phrases, clauses, or even sentences. There are two general types of conjunction:

28.1 COORDINATING

Coordinating conjunctions link words, phrases, clause, and sentences, like for like:

words: sings <u>and</u> dances

phrases: in the ballpark <u>but</u> out of fair territory

clauses: we don't swim <u>nor</u> do they sail

sentences: I quit the job. <u>For</u> I am weary and frustrated.[1]

Correlatives are a common type of coordinating conjunctions, where one correlative is found in each coordinate clause or phrase. The most common correlatives are 'both . . . and', 'either . . . or', 'neither . . . nor', 'not only . . . but also', 'on the one hand . . . on the other (hand)'.

28.2 SUBORDINATING

Subordinating conjunctions operate solely on the level of linking clauses: specifically, a main clause and a subordinate clause (see §3.2):

I will read the book, when you finish it.
[MAIN CLAUSE] [SUBORDINATE CLAUSE]

Just as my mother taught me, I always speak the truth.
[SUBORDINATE CLAUSE] [MAIN CLAUSE]

---

1. Starting about the mid-20th century, formal American English began to frown on the use of most sentence conjunctions; Latin, on the other hand, is fond of them.

In English, there is a much wider array of subordinating conjunctions than coordinating conjunctions, even though the latter are used in a greater variety of settings.

So too, in Latin, coordinating conjunctions are probably more frequent and widespread, while subordinating conjunctions are more specific in meaning and more numerous in variety. The most common coordinating (and correlative) conjunctions according to type are the following:

DISJUNCTIVE: *aut, vel, -ve* [enclitic]: or; *aut . . . aut, vel . . . vel, -ve . . . -ve:* either . . . or

ADVERSATIVE: *sed, verum, at, atqui, tamen, autem, vero:* but, yet, however, and yet, but yet

COPULATIVE: *et, -que* [enclitic]: and; *et . . . et, -que . . . -que, -que . . . et:* both . . . and; *nec . . . nec, neque . . . neque:* neither . . . nor

CAUSAL: *enim, etenim, nam, quippe:* for

CONSEQUENTIAL: *igitur, ergo, itaque, ideo, idcirco, proin, proinde, quare:* then, therefore, accordingly, so then, now then, so therefore

>*aut per terram aut per mare*
>either by land or by sea
>*iustus sed severus*
>just but harsh
>*nec in urbe nec in oppido*
>neither in the city nor in the town
>*est promptus. iuvenis enim est.*
>He is ready, for he is young.
>*cogito; ergo sum.*
>I think; therefore I am.

Some coordinating conjunctions, when they link sentences or clauses, can serve as particles (see §27).

The Latin subordinating conjunctions are far too numerous to list. Some are exclusively subordinating; others can also be used in coordination. They can be classified into the following taxonomy:

TEMPORAL: conjunctions meaning 'when', 'before', 'after', 'between', 'until', etc.; see §24.

CAUSAL: conjunctions meaning 'since', 'because', etc.; see §23.

CONCESSIVE: conjunctions meaning 'though', 'although', 'even though', 'even if', etc.; see §18.

COMPARATIVE: conjunctions meaning 'as', 'just as', 'in the same way as', 'according as', etc. Some Latin conjunctions are accompanied by the indicative mood: *ut* or *uti* 'as', 'just as'; *sicut* or *sicuti* 'just as'; *velut* or *veluti* 'as', 'so as', 'even as', 'just as'; *prout* 'according as', 'just as'; *praeut* 'as compared with'; *ceu* 'like as', 'just as'. Other conjunctions are used with the subjunctive: *tamquam* 'as if'; *quasi* 'as if'; *velut* or *veluti* 'as if', 'just as if'.

CONDITIONAL: conjunctions meaning 'if', 'provided that', 'so long as', 'unless', etc.; see §17.

FINAL or CONSECUTIVE: conjunctions meaning 'so that', 'in order that', 'such that', 'so as to', 'that', 'to', etc.; see §§20 and 21.

LOCATIVE: conjunctions meaning 'where', 'where from', 'to where', 'whence', 'whither', 'by way of which', etc.; see §19.

RELATIVE: pronominal conjunctions meaning 'who', 'which', 'whom', 'whose', 'of which', 'to whom', 'to which', etc.; see §19.

Relative conjunctions and some locative conjunctions also function as pronouns. Some of the other Latin subordinating conjunctions also serve as adverbs, especially sentence adverbs (see §26).

29. INTERJECTIONS

As noted in §2.9, **interjections** are grammatically and syntactically very loose elements that can be added to clauses or sentences to convey elevated emotions or emphasis.

The most notable feature of interjections in English is their potential placement in almost any position within a sentence or clause:

Dammit all, I wish that this day would end.

I wish, dammit all, that this day would end.

I wish that this day, dammit all, would end.

I wish that this day would end, dammit all.

Because Latin survives to us primarily as a literary language, and because interjections are found primarily in colloquial usage, we know relatively few Latin interjections. Expressing amazement are *ecce, ehem, en, o, papae,* and *vah* 'wow!', 'whoa!'. Expressing enjoyment are *euhoe, evae, evoe,* and *io* 'yay!', 'yippie!'. Expressing grief or sorrow are *a, ah, ai, eheu, heu,* and *vae* 'alas!'. The interjections used for hailing someone publicly are *eho, ehodum,* and *heus* 'hey!', 'yo!'; to hail quietly, *st* 'psst!' is used. The interjections of praise are *eia* and *euge* 'hooray!', 'bravo!'; dispraise is expressed with *phy* 'ugh!', 'yuck!'.

INDEX OF TERMS

See also the table of contents. A bolded number indicates the page where a definition for the term is provided.